Healthy Drinks

Healthy Drinks

Kathryn Hawkins

COURAGE
BOOKS

AN IMPRINT OF RUNNING PRESS
PHILADELPHIA • LONDON

A QUINTET BOOK

9 8 7 6 5 4 3 2 1

Digit on the right indicates the number of this printing

ISBN 0-7624-0102-8

Library of Congress
Cataloging-in-Publication Number 97-68287

This book was designed and produced by
Quintet Publishing Limited
6 Blundell Street
London N7 9BH

Creative Director: Richard Dewing
Art Director: Clare Reynolds
Designer: Isobel Gillan
Project Editor: Clare Hubbard
Editor: Jane Hurd-Cosgrave
Food Stylist: Kathryn Hawkins
Photographer: Tim Ferguson-Hill
Consultant Nutritionist: Iris Epstein

Typeset in Great Britain by
Central Southern Typesetters, Eastbourne
Manufactured in Singapore by Eray Scan Pte Ltd.

Published by Courage Books, an imprint of
Running Press Book Publishers
125 South Twenty-Second Street
Philadelphia, Pennsylvania 19103-4399

The publisher would like to thank
Waring Products DN Dynamics Corp. of America for
supplying the picture featured on page 10.

Because of the risk of salmonella poisoning, raw eggs
should not be served to the very young, the ill or elderly,
or to pregnant women.

Contents

Introduction

We all need to drink in order to stay alive—but as much as we are aware of what we should be eating for good health, we should also be concerned about the nutritional value of our liquid intake and its effect on our diet and general well-being.

Many of the ready-made drinks on the market today, whether in a can, bottle, or carton, or powdered drinks out of a jar or packet—even tea and coffee—are full of ingredients which are unnecessary and can be detrimental to our health: refined sugar in the form of sucrose, artificial sweeteners, various colors and flavorings, and caffeine are all ingredients that can be included in ready-made and powdered drinks without us being aware of it unless we make a point of reading the ingredients list. Some commercial milk shakes and yogurt drinks have relatively high proportions of fat and sugar as well, yet we rely on these drinks as thirst-quenchers and rehydrators, usually without a second thought to their nutritional composition. These products either have zero, or insignificant nutritional benefits.

Eating too much sugar is a major cause of tooth decay, especially when sugary foods and drinks are consumed frequently through the day. Although sugar provides us with energy, it is full of empty calories. A healthy diet should provide all the energy you need without eating sugar. An excessive energy-raising food intake leads to obesity and associated health risks. Unrefined cane sugar and honey do contain trace elements, which can be included sparingly in a healthy diet, yet it is much better to rely on the natural sugars in fruits as much as possible.

Similarly, although a small amount of fat in the diet is essential for good health, and makes food more palatable, a fat-rich diet not only leads to a person becoming overweight, but is also linked with a higher risk of heart disease. The fats found in milk shakes and yogurt drinks are usually derived from animal or dairy sources, and therefore contain more saturated fats. The intake of these fats should be kept to a minimum, as they increase cholesterol in the blood, which in turn increases the risk of developing heart disease.

Caffeine is a naturally occurring substance found in coffee, cocoa, tea, maté, and the cola bean. It is a diuretic and a mild stimulant, producing a "lift" that lessens tiredness and sleepiness. It depletes nutrient levels by its diuretic properties, which cause more nutrients to be flushed out in the urine and affects the body's ability to absorb iron. It stimulates the nervous system, kidneys, and heart and dilates the blood vessels. Caffeine can also be very addictive—heavy caffeine drinkers have been known to suffer from withdrawal symptoms such as headaches and irritability when cutting down.

There have been lots of studies carried out on the effects of artificial additives on the body. Food colorings have been linked to hyperactivity in children in some studies, for example, and side effects for the sensitive have ranged from gastric disorders to asthma and eczema in various tests. Even if you are not allergic to additives, it is worth examining your intake of artificial chemicals to see how you feel about putting unnatural substances into your body, considering the potential hidden damages that may be occurring.

So what are the alternatives to commercially-produced drinks and tea and coffee? There are plenty of choices for healthier drinks: fresh fruit and vegetable juices; herb, fruit, and flower teas; shakes and smoothies made with lower-fat ingredients; cocktails and punches; and tonics for vitality and other aspects of health. Whether you want a refreshing drink, something to take the edge off your appetite, an interesting alternative to alcohol at a social event, or an immediate "pick-me-up," there is something to suit every occasion, without having to resort to convenience drinks. So next time you reach for a fizzy drink because you're thirsty, do your body a favor and think about a healthier alternative.

The Benefits
of Healthy Drinks

Taking vitamin and mineral supplements has now become part of our routine as a safeguard to maintain good health. Although supplements can be very useful, they shouldn't take the place of a healthy, balanced diet full of nutrient-rich foods. Fresh fruits and vegetables eaten in their raw state, and juices made from them, are very nutritious, cleansing, and balancing for the whole body, and they also offer the greatest supply of vitamins and minerals. Drinking a glass of juice is so much tastier and more satisfying than taking a multivitamin tablet, and is much better for you than convenience products. Fruit and vegetables can also be blended with other healthy components to provide different flavors, textures, and drinks for any occasion.

Vitamins

Vitamins are organic compounds that are effective in very small amounts. The body can't make them for itself, yet they are vital for good health. Therefore, they have to be ingested daily, preferably from a natural source, for maximum benefit to the body, i.e. in the form of good fresh food. We need vitamins to energize the body's metabolism, and to stimulate its growth and repair mechanisms. A serious vitamin deficiency can lead to disease. Here is the range of vitamins found in fresh juices:

Vitamin A (retinol): Needed for growth and development, proper eyesight, and the maintenance of the skin. Carrots and green vegetables have the greatest quantities in the form of beta carotene, which is converted to vitamin A for use in the body by the liver.

Vitamin B-Complex: B1 (thiamin); B2 (riboflavin); B3 (niacin); B6 (pyridoxine); B12 (cobalamin); biotin; folic acid; and pantothenic acid—these vitamins work together to help with digestion, and aid resistance to infection. Whole grains are rich in these vitamins, and among fruit and vegetables, green vegetables, sprouting seeds, and citrus fruits contain the most significant amounts.

Vitamin C: An antioxidant (it is incapable of being destroyed by oxygen—see below). Helps the body to protect the nerves, glands, tissues, and joints from oxidation, and aids the absorption of iron. All fresh fruits and vegetables contain this vitamin.

Vitamin E: An antioxidant that aids in the function of the heart and the proper use of fatty acids. Whole grains, seeds, and nuts are good sources, as are green vegetables.

Antioxidants: There is an increasing body of information about the value of these vitamins and minerals. Research is being carried out on the protection by antioxidants against degenerative diseases, and their ability to stabilize "free radicals" (an atom or group of atoms containing at least one unpaired electron and existing for a brief period of time before reacting to produce a stable molecule). Free radicals react with molecules in our bodies and put our cells at risk, which in turn leads to degeneration in our bodies. They are generated by toxins which get into our bodies from pollution in the air.

Minerals

Minerals found in food sources are very different from those supplied by supplements. They are always accompanied by specific amino acids and vitamins, which the body recognizes and can put to use straight away. They help maintain our energy levels, nerves, muscles, hair, and bones. They keep the blood clean and at the right pH (acid/alkaline) balance. These are some of the minerals found in fruit juices, with a description of their direct action on the body.

Calcium: Maintains pH balance; strengthens teeth and bones.

Germanium: An antioxidant, it allegedly aids function of immune system, and helps reduce high-blood pressure.

Iodine: Enables the thyroid gland to maintain the body's metabolism.

Iron: Part of the blood: helps transport oxygen around the body for cell respiration, and for heart and lung operation.

Magnesium: Helps the body use proteins, produce energy, and keep the cells in good repair.

Manganese: Necessary for maintaining the body's nervous-system structure; activates enzymes concerned with energy release.

Phosphorus: A structural component to bones and teeth, which helps with energy release.

Potassium: Maintains the chemical balances in all the muscles, including the heart; aids energy production and maintains water balance in the cells.

Selenium: An antioxidant that works alongside vitamin E to delay oxidation of fatty acids.

Sodium: Works with potassium, calcium, and magnesium to neutralize acids, maintain water balance in the cells, and maintain cell and tissue energy.

Sulfur: An essential part of the body's function and general well being.

Other benefits

Juices and other health drinks are also valuable for the fluid they provide. Fluids in the form of fresh juices help cleanse the blood and transfer live plant energy to the body. They make you feel revived and "lifted", as they contain pure, naturally distilled water. Other beverages, such as tea, coffee, alcoholic drinks, fizzy and flavored soft drinks, and water from the faucet contain many impurities, which first have to be eliminated by the liver and kidneys before the pure fluid can be used, making these valuable organs work harder.

Because juices are liquid, they are quickly and easily digested in the stomach, and their nutrients absorbed into the bloodstream. Juices also contain plant enzymes that combine with the body's natural enzymes to aid digestion and the absorption of nutrients, and also help to neutralize excess proteins and fat from other foods. These enzymes are like an in-built construction team in the body, constantly rebuilding tissue after wear and tear. However, enzymes are extremely heat sensitive, and are destroyed during the cooking process. Therefore, only raw fruit and vegetables can supply these valuable substances.

Proteins are made up of chains called amino acids, and these are the body's "building blocks" that are responsible for cell renewal and many other functions. All fresh juices contain amino acids, but especially sprouting seeds and green, leafy vegetables. Amino-acid deficiency can cause allergies, weak immunity, and poor digestion.

In addition, all fruits contain acids that can help remove toxins from the digestive tract. Citrus fruits contain citric acid, which is the strongest; other fruits contain milder acids like malic and tartaric. Apples contain pectin, which also helps with the absorption of toxins and fats during digestion. Chlorophyll, found in green vegetables, is the substance which enables plants to harvest energy from the sun. Chlorophyll-rich food sources are spinach, watercress, parsley, celery, cucumber, lettuce, green bell peppers, scallions and kale.

Above all, it is important to remember that when you make yourself a healthy drink, you think about its combined ingredients in order to obtain as much nutrition as possible. You need to combine the fresh fruit and vegetable juices with equally healthy, natural foods so that you are not polluting the body with impurities. For example, use pure spring water or mineral water, or fruit and herb teas made with spring water. If you need to add a sweetener, use honey, maple syrup or unrefined sugars. Also, always use low-fat dairy products for milk shakes and smoothies, and substitute organically grown products wherever possible.

Equipment

Making your own drinks can easily become part of your daily routine, and there are various types of equipment on the market to help you save time and make your drink-making easier. The equipment divides roughly into two basic types: those that blend all parts together, and those that extract juice only. However, you can get started immediately without any specialist equipment, and this chapter describes all the equipment, methods, and tips to produce perfect results.

Blenders/Food Processors

These pieces of equipment are designed to liquidize whatever is put into them by shredding at a high speed. Blenders are best used for making drinks like cocktails, smoothies, and shakes that need to be well mixed together to give a smooth, even-textured result. It is worth bearing in mind that too much fiber in a drink can taste unpleasant; however, dietary fiber is important for health, and any fiber that you do keep in your drinks should be used as a part of your whole diet—make sure you also eat plenty of whole grains, cereals, and unrefined carbohydrate food like brown rice, pasta, and brown bread to give yourself plenty of bulk.

If you don't have a blender or food processor, then you can simply mash the ripe fruit with a fork and then mix it with the other ingredients. The result will be thicker and slightly less smooth, but still perfectly acceptable. You can also sift the fruit through a fine-mesh strainer, or for a finer result, strain it through a piece of clean cheesecloth.

Juicers

There are several different types of machines that will extract the juice from fruits and vegetables, without the need for prior separation of their various constituents. The machine you choose to buy should be judged by its capacity for juicing the fruits and vegetables you want to drink; how easy the machine is to put together and clean, its size for storage purposes; and, of course, the price. It goes without saying, that the more sophisticated the machine, the more expensive it will be. These are a few of the types of juicers available:

Centrifugal: An electrically powered, high-speed juicer that chops up the fruit or vegetables, and then spins at a high speed in a meshed basket. This in turn separates the juice from the pulp. The pulp remains in the basket and the juice is passed in to a separate container. Centrifugal juicers tend not to cope with large quantities of produce, and are usually at the cheaper end of the market. They should be cleaned regularly, otherwise they will get clogged up. The juice produced from this type of machine is thick and creamy, and the pulp is wet. Some models include a pulp ejector, which automatically discards the pulp through a side opening.

Masticating: This high-speed juicer can be manual or electric. It chops finely the fruit or vegetables into a paste and then squeezes out the juice through a mesh at the bottom. It is more efficient than a centrifugal juicer, and also more expensive. These models cope well with skin, peel, pips, and harder-skinned fruit and vegetables.

Hydraulic Press: This can be manual or electric. A very efficient high-speed juicer that chops finely the fruit and vegetables into a paste, then presses the paste under great pressure, resulting in a high-quality filtered juice and a dry pulp. These machines can cope with a large quantity of produce, but they do tend to be quite costly.

Citrus Juicers: These extract the juice from all citrus fruits. They can be electric, whereby the halved fruit is held on a cone and the machine turns, causing the extracted juice to fall into a container below. The pith and pips are held in a grid above. Alternatively, you can buy a manual juicer or a simple glass or plastic squeezer to do the job. The resulting juices from these types of equipment are much clearer and thinner than a juice made in another type of juicing machine.

Juicing by hand: On the whole, if you juice by hand, slightly less juice is produced than if you use an electric extractor. All you need is a grater, a bowl, a fine sieve, and some clean cheesecloth. Simply grate the fruit or vegetable into the bowl, and then place the grated produce in the center of the piece of cheesecloth, gather up the edges, and squeeze the contents as hard as possible through the sieve or if preferred, into the bowl. Sifting the juice provides a more superior result. The juice is then ready to drink or to use in a recipe.

Tips
for Making Healthy Drinks

So now you've learned what equipment can be used to help you in the kitchen, it is important to take a look at the following essential tips in order to make the highest-quality, most nutritious drinks possible:

Keep your drink-making equipment clean and dry to avoid contamination. If you have been using strongly flavored ingredients, make sure you rinse out the container thoroughly so that flavors don't get mixed up. Some juices may discolor the equipment, such as carrot or red cabbage; this will not affect the performance of the appliance. Some discolorations may be removed by carefully rubbing them with a cloth dipped in vegetable oil. Chopped apple put through the equipment is also a good cleanser—it helps to get rid of lingering odors and color staining.

Wherever possible, drink or use the juices immediately so as not to lose their valuable nutritional content. Some vitamins are easily destroyed by air and light. It is better to make a sufficient quantity of drink to suit your immediate needs—if you do need to store the juice, keep it for a few hours only in the refrigerator, and add a few drops of lemon juice to aid preservation. Digestion is improved by drinking fresh juices on an empty stomach—30 minutes before or after a meal, or as a between-meal snack.

Choose the best-quality produce possible for making your own drinks. Avoid wilted, bruised, and damaged fruit and vegetables lacking color. Look out for ripe, mature produce that will not only be easier to digest, but contains the most nutrients. Try to avoid buying in bulk if possible; it is better to purchase little and often to ensure maximum freshness. Check sell-by and use-by dates, and avoid using out-of-date produce for hygiene and safety reasons. If you're mixing juices with other ingredients in recipes, check that the additional foods are as natural as possible—always read the nutrition panels and ingredient labels on the package.

Organic fruit and vegetables will produce the most natural and uncontaminated drinks. They do tend to be more expensive, and there is less of a range than with standard varieties, but their advantage is that they have not been exposed to any chemical treatments or waxes during growth and transportation. Therefore, there will be no residues left on the skin, and this means you can safely use the whole fruit or vegetable without fear of ingesting a dose of chemicals. If you have to peel the produce before using it, you will significantly reduce the nutrient content, as many nutrients are contained in the thin skin. Thicker-skinned produce is not as easily affected, as the chemicals don't penetrate the inner flesh, and the skin is usually discarded.

Serving Suggestions

Once you've made your drinks, there are many ways that you can dress them up—this is especially good if you're serving them for a special party or social event. These decorations can range from the simple slice of relevant fruit or vegetable dangled or draped on the glass to the more elaborate cocktail umbrella, swizzle stick, or straw

Here are some more presentation ideas and serving tips:

Fresh herbs and edible flowers, such as pansies, nasturtiums, and primroses (check that any flowers you intend using have not been sprayed with toxic chemicals and always make sure that you have correctly identified the plant. If in doubt, don't use.) look good for a natural garnish, and cubes of fruit or vegetable threaded onto small skewers, toothpicks, or colorful swizzle sticks can add an extra dimension to the drink. Don't forget to wash the decoration or garnish before using.

Make sure you have plenty of ice for those summer days when you need a real thirst-quencher. Make your own cubes using mineral or spring water—you can also freeze small bits of fruit or herb in water in ice-cube trays for extra effect. Small quantities of juice can also be frozen in this way, and then added to other juices for a slow release of flavor. Freezing—providing it is soon after making the juice—doesn't affect the nutritional value of the juice. To make crushed ice, simply place cubes in a blender or food processor and crush for a few seconds until fine.

Place glasses in the freezer to frost for an extra-cold drink, this looks particularly effective if making a healthy cocktail. Rinse heatproof glasses and mugs with very hot water to heat them in advance for hot toddies and savory drinks—make sure the handle doesn't get too hot, though, as you won't be able to pick it up!

For that extra bit of professionalism, why not sugar-frost glasses? Simply rub the rim of the glass with a piece of fruit, then lightly dip the rim in a saucer of superfine granulated sugar. Or, use salt and lime in the same way, margarita-style.

Don't waste the peel or skin from citrus fruit—it can be cut into a wide variety of decorative shapes using small cookie cutters. If you carefully pare the peel from a citrus fruit using a peeler, the peel can be wound around a skewer or spoon handle, and then frozen to form a spiral. This is very simple, but looks impressive draped over a serving glass.

Fruits and Vegetables

Most healthy drinks included in this book will be based on the juices from fruit or vegetables. This list shows the main fruit and vegetables for juicing, and the properties of each, so you can choose which will be the most beneficial to you; however, it is not comprehensive, as other fruits or vegetables may be substituted.

General warnings

Start by drinking a small amount of juice every day, up to 10 fluid ounces to start with, and gradually build up the amount you consume. This will ensure that your body gets used to this concentrated form of nutrition.

Always dilute dark-green and dark-red vegetable juices by four parts to one, remembering that they are very potent cleansers.

Drinking too much fruit juice can give your system an overload of the fructose, natural sugar, found in fruit. If you suffer from sugar intolerance, diabetes, or candidiasis, you should be wary of the amount of fruit juice you drink.

A child's digestive system is more delicate than that of an adult. If you want to give fresh juices to children, remember to dilute the juice as their concentration is likely to be too strong. Avoid strong-flavored juices, and stick to the milder, sweeter ones until they get used to the different flavors.
This guide shows which fruit and vegetables can be blended, juiced, or both. The yield refers to the amount of juice produced if the food is juiced using a juice extractor. Bear in mind that if you blend the fruit or vegetable, the weight of the yield will be exactly the same as the weight of the whole fruit or vegetable as there is no waste, so the resulting juice will be much thicker than that produced in a juice extractor.

Berry fruits

BLACK CURRANT

A small, round, black fruit that gives a dark, strong-flavored juice. It mixes well with other juices, such as apple. Choose fresh or frozen organic fruits. Wash well, remove stalks, and juice. Blend or juice.
Nutrition: Rich in vitamins A (beta-carotene) and C, with smaller amounts of B3, pantothenic acid, biotin, and E. High in potassium and calcium, with good supplies of magnesium, phosphorus, iron, sulfur, and chlorine.
Benefits: The skins contain compounds that have the ability to inhibit the growth of harmful bacteria. The high vitamin C content has powerful antioxidant properties.
Yield: Approximately 7 fluid ounces of juice per 1 pound of whole fruit.

BLUEBERRY

A small, dark, blackish-blue, round fruit with a delicate, lightly scented juice. Choose any ripe, unblemished fruits—use fresh or frozen for juices. Simply wash well and use whole. Blend or juice.
Nutrition: Useful supplies of vitamins A (beta-carotene), B-complex, and C, and a good supply of potassium and calcium. Also provides magnesium, phosphorus, sulfur, and chlorine.

Benefits: Blueberries contain high concentrations of compounds in their skin that can destroy harmful bacteria in the digestive tract and help keep it clean and healthy.
Yield: Approximately 7 fluid ounces of juice per 1 pound of whole fruit.

CRANBERRY

A round, bright, pinky-red fruit with a slightly sour taste; it is acidic, and therefore best mixed with other, sweeter, fruit juices or ingredients. Choose deep-colored, firm fruit and wash well before using. Blend or juice.
Nutrition: A good source of vitamins A (beta-carotene), B complex, folic acid, and C, and minerals—potassium, calcium, magnesium, phosphorus, iron, and sulfur.
Benefits: A natural diuretic and urinary tract cleanser. Cranberries increase the urine's acidity, and thus help destroy bacteria.
Yield: Approximately 10 fluid ounces of juice per 1 pound of whole fruit.

RASPBERRY

A fresh, tart pinky-red berry. Raspberries are best blended as the yield of juice is very small, and therefore wasteful. If you want a smooth juice, sift out the seeds. Choose ripe, firm fruits that are unbruised. Simply wash well, remove the stalks, and blend only.
Nutrition: A good supply of vitamins C and folic acid, with smaller amounts of A (beta-carotene), B1, B2, B3, B6, pantothenic acid, and E. Raspberries contain potassium, calcium, magnesium, phosphorus, iron, zinc, sulfur, and chlorine.
Benefits: Excellent uplifting properties.

STRAWBERRY

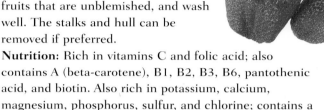

A bright red berry with a strongly scented flavor, and very thick in texture. It is best blended and mixed with other juices for drinking. Choose ripe, sweet-smelling fruits that are unblemished, and wash well. The stalks and hull can be removed if preferred.
Nutrition: Rich in vitamins C and folic acid; also contains A (beta-carotene), B1, B2, B3, B6, pantothenic acid, and biotin. Also rich in potassium, calcium, magnesium, phosphorus, sulfur, and chlorine; contains a smaller amount of iron.
Benefits: A good refreshing cleanser for the whole body, and a mild diuretic.

Citrus fruits

GRAPEFRUIT

A large, round citrus fruit; its color depends on the variety used. Pink and Ruby grapefruits are generally sweeter and slightly less acidic than white varieties. Choose heavy fruits with a thin skin. Peel the fruit, quarter, and discard the seeds. It is not necessary to remove all the pith before processing, as it will give a creamier juice with a more-nutritious content. If you use a citrus press, the pith will not be present. Blend or juice.

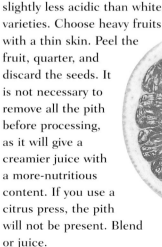

Nutrition: Pink varieties are particularly rich in vitamin A (beta-carotene); all are rich in C and folic acid, potassium, calcium, magnesium, phosphorus, sulfur, and chlorine.
Benefits: Pectin, which is an aid to circulatory and digestive problems, is found in the white pith and in the dividing segment membranes. This juice can also be beneficial for improving the skin.
Yield: Approximately 5 fluid ounces of juice per 1 pound of whole fruit.

LEMON

A small, oval-shaped, yellow citrus fruit with a very sharp-tasting, creamy juice. A little goes a long way as a mixer. Choose firm lemons with thin skins. Peel away the skin, and quarter. Pits can be removed if preferred. Blend or juice.
Nutrition: High in vitamin C, with a smaller supply of vitamin A (beta-carotene), B1, B2, B3, B6, and pantothenic acid, and minerals potassium, calcium, magnesium, phosphorus, and iron.
Benefits: Lemons have a well-known reputation as a cure for scurvy—a skin disease which results in a diet deficient of vitamin C. It is a good cleanser when drunk in small amounts before a meal. It is an effective antioxidant—when added to other fruit and vegetables, it can prevent discoloration and acts as a preservative.
Yield: Approximately 3½ fluid ounces of juice per 1 pound of whole fruit.

LIME

A dark green, oval-shaped fruit similar to lemon, but with weaker properties. The juice is quite sharp and acidic in flavor, and pale green in color. Again, only a small amount is needed as a mixer. Choose firm, heavy limes with thin skins for maximum yield. Peel away the skin, remove pits if preferred, and juice. Can be blended or juiced.

Nutrition: A good source of vitamin C, with smaller amounts of vitamin A (beta-carotene), B1, B2, B3, and pantothenic acid.
Benefits: Limes are slightly less acidic than lemons and so are not as powerful as a cleanser.
Yield: Approximately 5 fluid ounces of juice per 1 pound of whole fruit.

ORANGE

A fresh-tasting, orange-colored, well-rounded citrus fruit. The juice is creamy and pale orange in color if pith is used. Deeper color results if the blood variety is used. Choose firm, heavy juicing oranges with thin skins. Peel away skin leaving some pith, and remove pits if preferred. Blend or juice.

Nutrition: Blood oranges have the highest amount of vitamin A (beta-carotene), but all are rich in C and folic acid. There are smaller amounts of B1, B2, B3, B6, pantothenic acid and E. Oranges have a good supply of potassium, calcium, magnesium, phosphorus, sulfur, and chlorine, and a small amount of sodium.

Benefits: As with other citrus juices, oranges help to clean up the digestive system. Cells, capillaries, heart, and lungs benefit from the intake of orange juice, and it is also good for promoting healthy skin.

Yield: Approximately 5 fluid ounces of juice per 1 pound of whole fruit.

Green vegetables

ASPARAGUS

A fresh-tasting, bright-green vegetable. Choose either firm, young tips or larger, tender, whole asparagus. Wash well, trimming off hard ends, and juice.

Nutrition: Rich in vitamins A (beta-carotene), B1, B3, folic acid, and C. Smaller amounts of other B complex. High potassium, sulfur and chlorine content, with a good supply of calcium, magnesium, phosphorus, and zinc.

Benefits: A highly alkaline vegetable that helps lower the acid content of the blood. It is a good cleanser and diuretic, and helps break down oxalic acid in the kidneys and muscles.

Yield: 2 fluid ounces of juice per 8 ounces of whole vegetable.

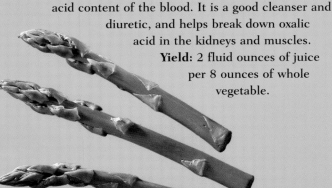

BELL PEPPER

A waxy-skinned vegetable of variable color—green, yellow, orange, or red. Red pepper gives the sweetest juice. Choose firm, unblemished peppers, and discard the stalk and seeds, if preferred. Wash well, chop, and juice.

Nutrition: Red bell pepper is very high in vitamin A (beta-carotene), and has more B3 than the green or yellow variety. Otherwise peppers provide a good supply of B6, C and folic acid, and the minerals potassium, phosphorus, iron, and chlorine.

Benefits: Has antioxidant properties, helps promote healthy skin.

Yield: Approximately 3½ fluid ounces of juice per 1 pound of whole vegetable.

BROCCOLI

A bright-green vegetable with a slightly bitter taste. It is best diluted when juiced. Choose dark-green flowerets with no yellowing, the buds should be tightly closed. Wash well, and then juice the flowerets and stalks.

Nutrition: An excellent source of vitamins A (beta-carotene), C, and folic acid. Also contains B1, B2, B3, B6, and E. High in potassium, calcium, phosphorus, iron, sulfur, chlorine, sodium, zinc, and magnesium.

Benefits: Has a high iron and vitamin C content. It helps carry oxygen to the blood.

Yield: Approximately 5 fluid ounces of juice per 1 pound of whole vegetable.

CABBAGE

A larger, round, multi-leaved vegetable which comes in many forms – they can be flat, conical, or round, the leaves curly or plain and different varieties of cabbage are different colors. Red cabbage produces a purple-colored juice with a mild peppery taste; it should be diluted before drinking. Green (Savoy) cabbage has a more pungent taste that is better mixed with a sweeter juice; the juice is dark green in color. White cabbage is much sweeter in taste, and pale green in color. Choose fresh, full, dense heads of cabbage. Discard outer leaves, wash, cut into chunks, and juice.
Nutrition: Savoy cabbage is very rich in vitamin A (beta-carotene), and is higher in folic acid and iron than other cabbages. In general, cabbage provides a useful quantity of vitamins B1, B3, B6, pantothenic acid, biotin, and C. It also provides potassium, phosphorus, zinc, sulfur, and chlorine. Cabbage also has a little sodium.
Benefits: A cleanser and stimulator of the immune system.
Yield: Approximately 5 fluid ounces of juice per 1 pound of whole vegetable.
Warning: Cabbage juice is more digestible if diluted, as it may cause mild digestive upset.

CELERY

A mild, refreshing, savory-tasting green watery vegetable. Adds good flavor to savory drinks. Choose firm and crisp stalks without wilting or damage. Wash them well and chop before juicing.
Nutrition: Useful amounts of vitamins A (beta-carotene), B3, folic acid, pantothenic acid, biotin, and E. Celery is rich in potassium, calcium, and chlorine; its "savory" taste is derived from its organic sodium content.
Benefits: Celery helps to eliminate waste from the kidneys, and can help ease sugar cravings.
Yield: Approximately 7 fluid ounces of juice per 1 pound of whole vegetable.

CUCUMBER

A long, green vegetable with a high water content that makes a refreshing juice that blends well with stronger juices. Choose unwaxed, firm, dark-green, medium-length cucumbers. Peel cucumbers that have been waxed; otherwise, wash them well and then blend or juice.
Nutrition: Useful amounts of vitamins A (beta carotene, however, note most is in the cucumber skin), B3, folic acid, pantothenic acid, biotin, potassium, calcium, phosphorus, iron, sulfur, and chlorine.
Benefits: Cucumber is a natural diuretic; also good for aiding skin rejuvenation.
Yield: Approximately 10 fluid ounces of juice per 1 pound of whole vegetable.

LEEK

A mild, onion-flavored, light-green colored, stalk vegetable. Adds flavor to savory drinks. Choose firm leeks with good color. Discard outer coarse leaves. Rinse well to remove grit and soil trapped between the leaves, and juice.
Nutrition: Rich in vitamins A (beta carotene), the B complex, and E; smaller amount of vitamin C. High content of potassium, and good amounts of calcium, phosphorus, iron, sulfur, and chlorine.
Benefits: A good cleanser and diuretic. Helps to eliminate uric acids, a build-up of which can lead to gout and painful joint inflammation.
Yield: Approximately 5 fluid ounces of juice per 1 pound of whole vegetable.

LETTUCE

A round, soft-leaved vegetable; its juice ranges from bright to dark green depending on variety used. Slightly bitter, strong taste that is better diluted with other juices to make it more palatable. Choose dark green varieties such as romaine or butterhead for a more nutritious juice. Heavy varieties yield more juice. Look for fresh, dense heads. Discard damaged leaves, chop, and juice.

Nutrition: On average, lettuce is rich in vitamin A (beta-carotene), potassium, calcium, and chlorine. There is also a useful supply of the B complex, E, phosphorus, iron, and sulfur.

Benefits: Rich in chlorophyll which is good for building up the blood, and helps promote healthy skin and hair.

Yield: Approximately 3½ fluid ounces of juice per 1 pound of whole vegetable.

SPINACH

A dark green, leafy vegetable that gives a strong-tasting juice; it must be diluted, and is best used in moderate amounts. Choose fresh, deep-green colored leaves with no sign of wilting. Wash well to remove grit, and blend or juice.

Nutrition: An excellent source of vitamins A (beta-carotene) and folic acid. Also present in smaller amounts are vitamins B1, B2, B3, B6, C, and E. Rich in potassium, calcium, magnesium, sodium, phosphorus, iron, zinc, sulfur, and chlorine.

Benefits: Rich in chlorophyll, so is good for the blood. A good cleanser, and a mild laxative.

Yield: Approximately 3½ fluid ounces of juice per 1 pound of whole vegetable.

Warning: Spinach contains oxalic acid, which inhibits calcium from being absorbed by the body when taken in excess.

Melons

A large, oval to round fruit with a hard skin and soft fleshy fruit belonging to the gourd family, as do squash and pumpkin. Yields a refreshing, aromatic juice that is best drunk on its own as it can ferment rapidly in the stomach. Color ranges from pale yellow to light orange depending on variety used. Do not choose melons with soft spots, they should be firm with a sweet smell. A heavy melon will yield more juice. Cut into slices and remove peel and pits, if preferred. Blend for best results.

Nutrition: Cantaloupe melon is high in vitamin A (beta-carotene), and honeydew is also a good supplier. Melons have a useful supply of the B complex and a little vitamin C. On average all melon varieties have a good supply of potassium, calcium, magnesium, phosphorus, and chlorine.

Benefits: Promotes a calming effect on the digestive system, with a mild stimulating action on the kidneys, and a gentle laxative effect.

WATERMELON

A large, oval to round fruit with a juicy red, crisp flesh and seeds. If using the flesh only, the juice is pink, but is browner and more nutritious if you use the skin as well. It has a very refreshing flavor, and a high-water content. Choose a well rounded fruit with a smooth, hard skin. If you are going to use the skin, wash it well. Chop up and then blend or juice. Pits should be used for a more nutritious drink.

Nutrition: Rich in vitamin A (beta-carotene), with useful amounts of B1, B2, B3, B6, folic acid, pantothenic acid, biotin, and C, and minerals potassium, calcium, magnesium, phosphorus, and iron.

Benefits: Watermelon is an excellent cleanser for the bladder and kidneys; it is also a mild diuretic, and is a natural appetite stimulator.

Yield: Approximately 10 fluid ounces of juice per 1 pound of whole fruit.

Orchard fruits

APPLE

A good, all-round fruit for juicing that mixes well with just about every other fruit and vegetable. It has a sweet, acidic flavor, and the color ranges from pale yellow to golden brown depending on whether the skin and pips are used. Choose firm, crisp, organic apples that won't need peeling. Just wash and chop roughly. Otherwise, an ordinary apple will have to be peeled. The core can be used if liked. Juice only.

Nutrition: A useful supply of vitamins A (beta-carotene), B1, B2, B6, C, biotin, and folic acid, and minerals calcium, potassium, magnesium, and phosphorus. However, if the apples are peeled, the amount of vitamin A is greatly reduced.

Benefits: The pectin in apple skin and the vitamin C help keep cholesterol stable; pectin also slows down the stomach's emptying, regulates bowel movements, and helps the body in digesting and eliminating toxic waste matter. The malic acid and tartaric-acid content help relieve indigestion, and help break down fatty foods and excess proteins. An excellent appetite suppressor if you're on a fat-reducing diet.

Yield: Approximately 10 fluid ounces of juice per 1 pound of whole fruit.

APRICOT

A light-orange-colored fruit with a fairly sweet taste. Choose ripe, unblemished, golden-orange organic fruit. Wash well, halve, and pit before using. Blend only.
Nutrition: An excellent supply of vitamin A (beta-carotene); useful amounts of vitamins C, B3, folic acid, and pantothenic acid, and minerals potassium, calcium, magnesium, sulfur, and phosphorus.
Benefits: Owing to the high proportion of vitamin A (beta-carotene), this is an excellent juice for helping fight infection.

AVOCADO PEAR

A light, yellow-green fruit that is too oily to be juiced, and should instead be blended to obtain a lusciously thick and creamy mixture. Choose ripe fruit that gives slightly when lightly squeezed. Peel and pit before blending, and add lemon juice to prevent discoloration. Mix with other ingredients to drink, as it is very thick and rich. Blend only.
Nutrition: A high-fat fruit with useful amounts of vitamins A (beta-carotene), C, and E, and smaller amounts of the B complex. Also rich in potassium, with good supplies of calcium, magnesium, phosphorus, zinc, and sulfur.
Benefits: An excellent fruit for a high-energy drink.

CHERRY

A small, round fruit with a color ranging from yellow/orange to deep pink to dark red. It gives a delicious, sweet-tasting juice that is rich in flavor; it is best mixed with other ingredients. Choose deep, dark-colored, ripe cherries that are firm to the touch. Cherry juice is time-consuming to make, as the cherries must be washed, de-stalked, and pitted before using. Blend or juice.
Nutrition: A good source of vitamins A (beta-carotene) and C, plus useful amounts of B3, folic acid, and biotin, and minerals potassium, calcium, magnesium, phosphorus, and sulfur.
Benefits: A very alkaline juice which can help reduce the acidity of the blood.
Yield: Approximately 10 fluid ounces of juice per 1 pound of whole fruit.

PEACH (AND NECTARINE)

Rich golden-orange-colored fruits that give a sweet, thick juice with a deliciously fragrant and flowery taste. Choose deep-colored fruits that give a little when gently pressed. Wash well, halve, and remove the pit. Blend only.
Nutrition: Peaches and nectarines are very similar nutritionally. They have a good supply of vitamins A (beta-carotene) and C, with useful quantities of the B complex. Minerals include potassium, calcium, magnesium, phosphorus, iron, and sulfur.
Benefits: Peaches and nectarines are cleansing to the intestine, and help stimulate bowel movements.

PEAR

A distinctively shaped fruit with variously colored, thin skins; it gives a sweet, mild tasting juice, which can vary in thickness. If too thick, mix with other ingredients. A little lemon juice added to the freshly prepared pear juice will prevent discoloration. Any variety can be used. Look for a rich-colored fruit that is firm and unblemished. Organic varieties are preferable as the whole fruit, minus the stalk, should be used. Wash well, and juice or blend.

Nutrition: All pear varieties contain vitamins A (beta-carotene), B1, B2, B3, B6, folic acid, biotin, and C; and minerals potassium, calcium, magnesium, phosphorus, iron, and sulfur. .

Benefits: A mild diuretic and laxative.

Yield: Approximately 7 fluid ounces of juice per 1 pound of whole fruit.

Plants and sprouts

ALFALFA

A sprouting plant with a mild, nutty flavor, pale in color. It should be mixed with other juices. Choose fresh sprouts with small green leaves and store in the refrigerator. They are easy to grow, and use for yourself—simply wash and juice them.

Nutrition: A useful supply of vitamins A (beta-carotene), B complex, and C, and minerals potassium, calcium, magnesium, phosphorus, iron, and zinc.

Benefits: A rich supply of chlorophyll and amino acids. Alfalfa sprouts are one of the most nutritionally valuable plants we can eat.

Yield: Approximately 3½ fluid ounces of juice per 8 ounces of sprouts.

BEAN SPROUTS (BEAN SHOOTS)

A sprouting plant with a watery, cloudy liquid, and an earthy taste. It is best mixed with other juices. Choose clean, crisp-looking white shoots without leaves. Sprouts from aduki bean, mung bean, or lentils are suitable. Simply wash and juice.

Nutrition: Useful amounts of vitamins A (beta-carotene), B1, B2, B3, and C. High in potassium, and a good source of calcium, iron, and sodium.

Benefits: Rich in high-quality protein, and good for building the blood as they contain both vitamin C and iron—particularly lentil sprouts—enabling the body to absorb more iron than it would without the vitamin.

Yield: Approximately 3½ fluid ounces of juice per 8 ounces of sprouts (shoots).

FENNEL

A plant with a rich licorice-like, slightly sweet flavor; it gives a delicious aroma and is very pale green in color. Choose firm, fresh stalks; wash well, chop, and juice only.

Nutrition: A good source of vitamins A (beta-carotene), B1, B3, folic acid, potassium, calcium, phosphorus, zinc, chlorine, and iron, with a smaller amount of sodium.

Benefits: Particularly calming and soothing effect on the body.
Yield: Approximately 7 fluid ounces of juice per 1 pound of whole vegetable.

WATERCRESS

A deep-green-colored plant with small, crisp leaves and a pleasant, peppery, spicy taste. It must be diluted with other ingredients. Available all year-round, choose fresh, green leaves; rinse well and juice.
Nutrition: Rich in vitamins A (beta-carotene), C, and E, with good amounts of B1, B3, B6, pantothenic acid, and biotin.
Benefits: A powerful cleanser and an excellent source of chlorophyll.
Yield: Approximately 1 fluid ounce of juice per 4 ounces of whole vegetable.

Root vegetables

BEET

A very potent, deep-purple vegetable; its juice must be mixed with other juices. Choose smallish, firm roots and trim the tops—these can be juiced separately. Wash and scrub any soil or sand off before juicing.

Nutrition: High in folic acid, with smaller amounts of vitamins A (beta-carotene), B1, B2, B3, pantothenic acid, and C. Contains an abundance of minerals: high in potassium, sodium, calcium, phosphorus, iron, and chlorine, with smaller amounts of magnesium, zinc, and sulfur.
Benefits: A powerful cleanser and tonic.

Warning: taken on its own, the cleansing action can be so great that it can cause nausea and stomach upset. Always mix with other juices and ingredients to dilute it.

Yield: Approximately 7 fluid ounces of juice per 1 pound of whole vegetable.

CARROT

A bright-orange vegetable with a sweet, mild flavor that mixes well with other fruit and vegetable juices. Choose large, firm carrots with a deep, even orange color; check that there are no spade marks or disease. Scrub well, wash, remove tops, and chop before juicing.

Nutrition: Extremely high content of vitamin A (beta-carotene), with useful quantities of B1, B3, B6, folic acid, and pantothenic acid. Carrots also contain small amounts of sodium, potassium, calcium, phosphorus, iron, sulfur, and chlorine.
Benefits: An excellent tonic and rejuvenator. Carrot juice stimulates the digestion and is a mild diuretic.
Yield: Approximately 7 fluid ounces of juice per 1 pound of whole vegetable.

ONION

A small vegetable with a papery, thin, brown skin concealing layers of pungent white flesh. Gives a very strong-flavored juice that is better mixed with other savory juices. It is creamy in color. Choose firm onions, free from rot or mold. Peel off brown papery skin, chop, and finely blend or juice.
Nutrition: Useful amounts of vitamins B1, B3, B6, folic acid, biotin, and E. Good source of potassium, calcium, phosphorus, sulfur, and chlorine.
Benefits: Diuretic properties, beneficial for the circulation and respiration.
Yield: Approximately 7 fluid ounces of juice per 1 pound of whole vegetable.

PARSNIP

A root vegetable that gives a strong, sweet-flavored, cream-colored juice. Best mixed with other savory juices. Choose vegetables with large, firm roots. Discard earthy stalk ends, scrub well, chop, and juice.
Nutrition: Rich in folic acid, with good quantities of B1, B3, pantothenic acid, and vitamin E. Rich in potassium, calcium, phosphorus, and chlorine, with smaller amounts of magnesium, iron, zinc, sulfur, and sodium.
Benefits: Helps promote healthy skin, hair, and nails.
Yield: Approximately 5 fluid ounces of juice per 1 pound of whole vegetable.

RADISH

A deep-red root vegetable with a pale, pink-colored flesh and a pungent peppery taste. Should always be mixed with other vegetable juices. Choose fresh-looking red radishes; wash well and juice.
Nutrition: Useful amounts of vitamins B1, B3, folic acid, pantothenic acid, and C. Rich in potassium, with calcium, phosphorus, iron, sulfur, chlorine, and sodium in smaller amounts.
Benefits: Cleansing and soothing when taken in small amounts.
Yield: Approximately 2 fluid ounces of juice per 8 ounces of whole vegetable.

Warning: Excessive intake can irritate rather than soothe.

TURNIP

A root vegetable, usually of pale, yellowish-white color, and a distinct peppery taste. Choose firm turnips free of spade marks, and remove earthy stalks. Scrub well and chop before juicing.
Nutrition: A good source of folic acid, with smaller amounts of B1, B3, pantothenic acid, and C. High in potassium, calcium, phosphorus, and chlorine, with smaller amounts of sodium and sulfur.
Benefits: A traditional treatment for aiding in the elimination of uric acid.
Yield: Approximately 3½ fluid ounces of juice per 1 pound of whole vegetable.

Tropical fruits

BANANA

A thick, pale-yellow fruit that is also better to blend rather than juice, as it gives a rich, sweet, creamy mixture. Choose ripe, yellow fruits and simply peel and blend or mash them, then mix with other juices or ingredients—it is too thick to drink on its own.
Nutrition: A good supply of vitamin A (beta-carotene), and useful amounts of vitamins E, B3, folic acid, biotin, and C. A rich supply of potassium, and a good supply of magnesium, phosphorus, sulfur, and chlorine.
Benefits: Easily digested when ripe, bananas are an excellent aid to digestion. This rich potassium supply gives a real boost to our body's maintenance program.

KIWI FRUIT

A small, oval-shaped bright-green fruit with a thin, fuzzy outer skin, a sweet flavor, and a pulpy, thick texture. It is a good mixer, and is best blended. Choose firm, unblemished fruit. Peel away the skin and cut into quarters, Blend only.
Nutrition: An excellent source of vitamin C, and a good supplier of vitamin A (beta-carotene); kiwi fruits also include potassium, calcium, magnesium, phosphorus, sulfur, and chlorine.
Benefits: A wealth of vitamin C and potassium are the two main advantages of this small fruit. Its properties are good for circulation, digestion, and the skin, and they help give the body's system a boost.

MANGO

A green-and-red-skinned fruit with a tangy orange-colored flesh that gives a very thick, fragrant juice that should be mixed in order to drink. Like the banana, it is better blended. Choose firm fruits which give slightly when gently squeezed. Peel and slice the flesh away from the pit, and then process. Blend only.
Nutrition: Mangoes are very high in vitamin A (beta-carotene), with a good supply of vitamin C, and smaller amounts of B1, B2, B3, and E. They also have a good supply of potassium, calcium, magnesium, phosphorus, and iron.
Benefits: An excellent fruit for energy and vitality, and promoting healthy skin.

PAPAYA

An exotic fruit whose juice is peachy pink in color and thick in texture, with a sweet, fragrant flavor. It requires diluting with other ingredients, and is best blended. Fruits with a golden-yellow skin denote ripeness. They should give a little when lightly squeezed. Cut in half and scoop out seeds if preferred. Peel away the skin. Blend only.

Nutrition: High in vitamins A (beta-carotene) and C, with a useful supply of the B complex, potassium, calcium, magnesium, phosphorus, sulfur, chlorine, and a small amount of sodium.
Benefits: Papaya contains several enzymes, principally papain, which helps with the digestion of proteins. It is a real energy booster to the body, and it also helps stimulate the appetite, has a laxative effect, and is a good cleanser for the internal organs.

PINEAPPLE

A large, spiky-skinned fruit, rich golden yellow in color, with a sweet, thirst-quenching juice. Choose pineapples that have a golden skin, a prominent sweet smell, and that give a little when pressed. A ripe pineapple will allow a leaf to be pulled easily from its crown. Remove top and bottom and slice off the skin. Blend or juice.
Nutrition: A good supply of vitamin C, and smaller amounts of A (beta-carotene) and the B complex. Rich in potassium and chlorine, with smaller amounts of calcium, magnesium, phosphorus, and sulfur.
Benefits: Contains the enzyme bromelain, which aids the digestion of protein.
Yield: Approximately 5 fluid ounces of juice per 1 pound of whole fruit.

Vine fruits

GRAPE

A small, clustered fruit that is sweet and tangy in taste. The juice is pale green or dark pink in color, depending on the variety used; and it is also quite thick. If preferred, dilute juice with spring water to taste. Any sweet variety of grape can be used, as long as they are fresh and firm. Simply wash well, pull out the stalks, and use—seeds can be left in. Blend or juice.
Nutrition: A good supply of vitamins A (beta-carotene), B3, B6, folic acid, biotin, and C; and minerals potassium, calcium, magnesium, phosphorus, and sulfur.
Benefits: An excellent metabolism stimulator. Grapes are best taken on their own because they ferment quickly in the stomach if held back by other foods.
Yield: Approximately 10 fluid ounces of juice per 1 pound of whole fruit.

TOMATO

A round, tangy fruit, orangey-red in color with a slightly pink tinge and waxy, thin skin. Very fresh tasting; delicious on its own or as a mixer. Choose vine-ripened, red tomatoes. Wash well, de-stalk, and blend or juice.
Nutrition: High in vitamin A (beta-carotene), with good amounts of B3, folic acid, C, and E. Also a good supply of potassium, iron, and chlorine, with smaller amounts of sodium and sulfur.
Benefits: Helps stimulate circulation and has slight alkalizing properties.
Yield: Approximately 10 fluid ounces of juice per 1 pound of whole fruit.

Additional Ingredients

As well as fruit and vegetable juices, there are plenty of other ingredients that you can add to your drinks to make them more nutritious and suitable for your specific requirements.

BEE POLLEN

A mixture of bee saliva, plant nectar, and pollen, which is the male fertilizing powder discharged from flowers. It is collected from bee hives, and sold as loose powder, grains or tablets. It can easily be incorporated into drinks, or sprinkled over cereals.

Bee pollen is highly nutritious and revitalizing, containing plenty of protein and essential amino acids, potassium, magnesium, phosphorus, calcium, and iron, plus smaller amounts of vitamins B1, B2, pantothenic acid, biotin, C, and A (beta-carotene). It is usually taken by the spoonful, and can be quite expensive.

Note: It can cause an allergic reaction in pollen-sensitive individuals, so check before serving to guests.

BREWERS' YEAST

A by-product of beer brewing. It is exceptionally rich in the B-complex vitamins, with high levels of iron, zinc, magnesium, and potassium, and also provides protein. It is available in pill form or as a powder, which is more suitable for drink-making. It is highly concentrated, and is an excellent pick-me-up. The flavor is very strong, so it needs to be mixed carefully with other ingredients such as yogurt, juices, milk, and honey.

Note: It is high in purines, so should be avoided by gout sufferers.

HONEY

A sweet, heavy liquid produced by bees from the nectar of flowers. It has been used as both a food and medicine for thousands of years.

The nutritional content varies between different honeys. All honey consists of about 25% water; the rest is glucose and a little fructose. Most honey contains traces of minerals and vitamins B2 and B3. Although honey is better for you weight for weight than refined sugar, it's still an energy provider, and not much else, so should only be used in restricted amounts. However, honey also has antiseptic properties, is easy to swallow, and is soothing and calming.

NUTS

The dried fruit of various trees, which come cased in a protective shell. Like seeds, they grow into plants and trees, and so are richly packed with nutrients and nourishment. They are one of the most concentrated forms of protein available, as they contain vitamins B1, B6, and E, and minerals such as iron, potassium, magnesium, phosphorus, calcium, and zinc.

OATS

Oats are an easy-to-grow cereal even in cold and harsh climates. They are sold in the form of whole grain, rolled or flaked, or ground, as oatmeal bran.

They are an exceptionally rich grain—high in protein, potassium, calcium, phosphorus, iron, and zinc; they also contain several B vitamins, vitamin E, and some fat, mostly polyunsaturated. They are also easy to digest, with an ability to help soothe the stomach and digestive system.

Traditionally, oats have been made into possets and caudles, even gruel, and served in the sick room to aid and speed recovery.

Note: oats should be avoided by those on a gluten-free diet.

SEEDS

The mature fertilized ovules of certain flowering plants, are eaten for their flavor, texture and nutritional content (this varies with individual seeds). Seeds are best purchased in

They also have a high-fat content, which means that they go rancid quite quickly and so can become dangerous. It is best to eat them as freshly as possible, and store them in the refrigerator for as little time as possible. The fat in nuts is mostly polyunsaturated; however, coconut contains a high proportion of saturated fat, and Brazil and macadamia nuts also have a fairly high amount.

Mass production has resulted in many nuts being treated with preservatives and dyes, and most are salted and fried. Choose organic nuts that are unroasted and free from salt.

Almonds are high in oxalic and phytic acid, which combine with certain minerals and eliminate them from the body. Make sure plenty of vitamin C-rich foods are eaten at the same time to counteract this process. However, the oil in almonds is particularly soothing and sustaining, and can help ease digestive upsets.

Nuts should only be crushed or chopped just prior to using.

small amounts. Like nuts, they can easily become rancid and stale. Store them in an airtight container in a cool place. Do not crush or chop them until just ready to use. The following are types of seeds and their properties, which may be added to enhance healthy drinks:

Pumpkin: Flat green seeds taken from the inside of pumpkin gourds. The seeds are commonly known as pepitas and have a deliciously delicate flavor. High in protein, potassium, magnesium, phosphorus, iron, and zinc, with a useful supply of B1, B2, and B3 vitamins. They are also rich in polyunsaturated fat.

Sesame: Tiny seeds of an easy-to-grow annual plant that is widespread across the Middle and Far East. They have a nutty, slightly sweet flavor. Very high in calcium, they are a boon for anyone who doesn't eat dairy foods, and for vegetarians and vegans (those who use no animal products). They contain a good amount of protein, polyunsaturated fat, vitamins B1, B3, B6, folic acid, pantothenic acid, biotin, and E. Minerals include a good supply of potassium, magnesium, phosphorus, iron, and zinc. They are also rich in amino acids, which help keep the liver and kidneys healthy. In the Middle East, sesame seeds are believed to enhance and maintain sexual vigor.

Sunflower: Obtained from the center of dried sunflower heads. A good source of protein and B-complex vitamins. They are high in vitamin E, potassium, magnesium, and phosphorus, with smaller amounts of iron and zinc. They are also rich in polyunsaturated fat. Eaten regularly, sunflower seeds help give a boost to the system.

WHEAT BRAN

The outside of the wheat grain is removed during milling. It contains a high proportion of dietary fiber. It also has some starch and protein. Fiber enables the digestive system to function effectively, and is therefore essential for good health. It adds bulk to the diet, and is very filling. Bland tasting but crunchy in texture, it can be added to most dishes.

Note: Keep consumption to moderate levels, as it can prevent certain minerals from being absorbed.

WHEAT GERM

The tiny embryos of wheat grains that contain all the nutrients to grow a new plant. It is highly perishable, and is usually removed from commercially produced white flour to extend its shelf life. Wheat germ is available in various forms—raw, unprocessed, stabilized, (a treatment to stop rancidity, which reduces nutrients in the process); and toasted—some with sweetening added to keep from perishing.

Nutritionally, wheat germ is rich in B vitamins, particularly B6 and folic acid. It is also high in vitamin E, potassium, magnesium, phosphorus, iron, zinc, and chlorine. It has a mild flavor and is easy to digest, so is perfect for adding to a variety of dishes, including drinks. Once the pack has been opened, store in an airtight container and keep in the refrigerator.

YOGURT

Made from milk that has been treated with bacterial cultures, yogurt is a thick, creamy substance that is versatile, inexpensive, and one of the finest natural foods available. It has been widely used all over the world for many years.

It can be made from whole or skim milk, left natural, or flavored—always check the labels for added ingredients, such as artificial colors, flavorings, and sugars. Greek yogurt is a variety that has been strained, and is more concentrated and creamy. If you are sensitive to cow's milk, then look for goat's, ewe's, or soy-milk varieties.

Yogurt is a good source of protein, and low-fat varieties are especially recommended. It is high in calcium and other minerals like potassium and magnesium, and the B-vitamin complex.

"Live" yogurt contains a microbe called *Lactobacillus Bulgaricus* that helps to restore an equal balance between good and bad bacteria in the digestive tract, and helps combat stomach upsets and diarrhea. The lactic acids also aid the body's use of B vitamins and other nutrients like calcium. These acids are easier to digest than those in milk, and therefore many who are lactose-intolerant are able to substitute yogurt. Eating "live" yogurt is particularly beneficial when taking antibiotics that destroy bacteria in the digestive tract.

EGGS

Eggs can be added to drinks to give extra protein and substance, but should be omitted if the drinks are to be made for the elderly, young, babies, pregnant women, or people with immune-deficient systems, as they may contain salmonella. Cooking eggs will eliminate the risk of salmonella poisoning, but as most drinks will use raw or lightly cooked eggs, the above considerations must be heeded during preparation.

Eggs also have a high-cholesterol content, and should also be avoided by those on a cholesterol-free diet or with limited cholesterol intake. Always use fresh, unblemished eggs—preferably the free-range variety—and ensure that no shell particles are accidentally included in the drink.

Herbs and spices

The perfect way to "pep up" your healthy drinks is to add some fresh herbs or ground spices. Not only do they add flavor and aroma, but they also have their own special properties and nutrients. Here are some examples of the most commonly used:

BASIL

A highly aromatic herb, calming to the nerves and an aid to digestion.

CARAWAY

A well-known aid to digestion, which promotes appetite, sweetens the breath and helps relieves flatulence.

CHILE PEPPER

Fresh chiles are pungent and beneficial to the respiratory and circulatory system.

◂ CHIVES

Vivid green, hollow stems, chives have a mild onion flavor. Similar effect to onion and garlic, in that it stimulates the appetite and promotes digestion, and is also used as a mild laxative.

CILANTRO

The whole plant of this herb can be used, from the delicate, aromatic leaves to the stems, roots, and seeds. The leaves add a cooling quality to hot, pungent foods, and the seeds both aid digestion and act as a mild sedative.

CINNAMON

Has delicate, warming properties, and is perfect in a hot toddy for relieving lethargy. Contains antiseptic properties.

CLOVES

Clove "berries" are also warming, and give a boost to the system; they are mildly antiseptic.

CUMIN

Aromatic and nutty-flavored. This spice also has warming qualities; helps relieve flatulence.

DILL

A delicate-flavored herb; both the leaves and seeds are used. Helps to relieve indigestion, stomach cramps, insomnia, and colic.

GARLIC

A bulbous herb that is one of the earliest-used substances in medicine and cookery. It is believed to cleanse the blood and helps reduce cholesterol.

Garlic has antibacterial, antifungal, and antiviral properties, and contains the antioxidant germanium. It has a pungent odor, owing to the sulfur-containing compounds in its essential oil.

For maximum effect, garlic should be used in its freshest form. Simply peel away the outer, papery skin, and then crush or blend into savory drinks.

GINGER

A warming, antiseptic spice. Use the fresh root only to help relieve nausea, travel sickness, and colds. Also used to aid digestion.

GINSENG

A herbal product derived from the roots of the ginseng plant. It is grown in Russia, Korea, and China, and has been used for centuries to treat many ailments. Korean and Siberian ginsengs come from the same family, but have a different genus, although their properties are much the same.

Ginseng has a reputation as a universal cure-all, aphrodisiac, and elixir. It contains ginsenosides, which appear to stimulate the hormones and adapt to an individual's needs. Like garlic, it contains a high level of the trace mineral germanium, a powerful antioxidant. It can be chewed or taken as a drink or powder.

Note: ginseng should be avoided by people with hypertension.

MINT

A popular Middle-Eastern digestive; it stimulates the heart and nerves.

NUTMEG

A sweet, warming spice with a mild, uplifting effect. Can aid with digestion.

Note: Nutmeg should not be consumed in large quantities as it has hallucinogenic properties.

PARSLEY

A herb rich in vitamin A (beta-carotene) and C, with iron, calcium, potassium, and chlorophyll. It is a diuretic that is also good for the skin and can freshen the breath. It helps eliminate uric acid.

ROSEMARY

An herb that aids the digestion of fat. It stimulates the circulation, is a good "pick-me-up," and can help ease aching joints.

SAGE

An antiseptic, antifungal herb that helps aid digestion. Can help ease stress, as it stimulates the central nervous system.

Always use fresh herbs. Wash them well, chop, and simply sprinkle over drinks, or blend them in with other ingredients to add pungency and flavor. Keep your spices in a dark, cool, dry place for maximum preservation of color and flavor. Store all spices in airtight containers, and only use them when fresh—spices opened for more than three months will lose their potency.

Understanding Nutritional Analysis

It is vital to recognize the nutritional value of what we drink, therefore each recipe that follows is accompanied by nutritional analysis. Some of the most important nutrients essential to maintaining health are included and the calorie content of each drink is also assessed. Most of the terms are very familiar to us as we are used to seeing them on food packaging, but below are explanations of the more unusual terms and abbreviations used. The analysis has been based upon each recipe yielding enough for one serving; multiply quantities accordingly if you need to increase the quantity of drink produced.

(N) 152.9 *kcalories* • *protein* 2.475g • *carbohydrate* 37.05g • *fat* 1.446g • *dietary fiber* 12.01g • *vit. A* 31.22 **RE** • *folate* 71.54**ug** • *vit. C* 124.4mg • *potassium* 546mg • *calcium* 61.85mg.

RE stands for retinol equivalent which is the form of vitamin A which is completely absorbed by the body.

Folate is one of the B complex vitamins. The body needs it to help make genetic materials DNA and RNA and manufacture blood cells.

ug is the abbreviation for a microgram, which is a thousandth of a milligram. It is used in nutritional analysis as it enables a more accurate measurement to be given.

Healthy Drinks

Fruit Juices *sweet, zesty, refreshing,*

fragrant **Shakes and Smoothies** *luscious,*

thick, creamy, satisfying **Cocktails and**

Punches *cooling, tangy, relaxing, flavorsome*

High-Energy Drinks and Tonics *energizing,*

vital, uplifting, nourishing

Fruit Juices

Any of these juice combinations can be drunk as they are or diluted with mineral water, if preferred. They make a perfect between-meal snack or refreshing drink. The quantities are approximate, as these will depend on the produce and methods chosen. Juices that are blended are thicker than those made using an extractor, as these tend to be thinner, clearer, and yield less. All the recipes given below yield enough for one serving.

Mixed Berry

A sweet-tasting juice, which is deep-pink-colored. The perfect summer cleanser. It is best blended for maximum yield and little waste.

Makes approx. 1¼ cups/½ pint

1 cup/4 oz. strawberries
½ cup/2 oz. raspberries
½ cup/2 oz. blueberries
½ cup/2 oz. blackberries

Wash and hull the fruits, setting aside a few berries for decoration. Blend all the remaining fruits together. Pour over ice in a serving glass. Thread the reserved fruits onto a small skewer or toothpick and serve with the juice.

Ⓝ 152.9 kcalories • protein 2.475g • carbohydrate 37.05g • fat 1.446g • dietary fiber 12.01g • vit. A 31.22 RE • folate 71.54ug • vit. C 124.4mg • potassium 546mg • calcium 61.85mg.

Strawberry *and Apple*

A peachy pink, creamy juice that acts as an appetite suppressor and cleanser.

Makes approx. 1¼ cups/½ pint

2 apples
1½ cups/6 oz. strawberries
Strawberry leaves to decorate

Ⓝ 213.1 *kcalories • protein* 1.748g *• carbohydrate* 53.75g *• fat* 1.621g *• dietary fiber* 10.01g *• vit. A* 16.95 RE *• folate* 40.62ug *• vit. C* 137mg *• potassium* 660.5mg *• calcium* 41.59mg.

Wash the apples. Remove stalk, core, and peel. Then juice the prepared apples. Wash and hull the strawberries, reserving one for decoration. Blend the strawberries with the apple juice. Transfer to a glass. Slit reserved strawberry so it will sit on the edge of the glass, decorate with leaves, and serve.

Citrus

Creamy, pale orange/yellow in color, with a tangy, zesty flavor. A good internal and skin cleanser.

Makes approx. 1 cup/8 fl. oz.

2 large oranges
1 lemon
1 lime
Orange, lemon, and lime peel

Peel fruits, leaving some white pith, and blend or juice—remove pits if preferred. Alternatively, if using a citrus press or juicer, simply halve the fruits, and then juice. Serve decorated with citrus peel.

Ⓝ 160.1 *kcalories • protein* 3.567g *• carbohydrate* 43.27g *• fat* 0.622g *• dietary fiber* 9.780g *• vit. A* 57.41 RE *• folate* 91.04ug *• vit. C* 189.6mg *• potassium* 622.3mg *• calcium* 142mg.

Left **Citrus**

Exotic Fruit

Greenish-yellow color with black flecks; thick in texture. A filling, fresh, sweet, refreshing flavor. Beneficial for the digestive system and a good pick-me-up.

Makes approx. 2¼ cups/18 fl. oz.

½ medium-sized pineapple
1 small or "mini" mango
1 kiwi fruit

Peel the pineapple and chop roughly. Peel the mango and slice the flesh off the pit. Peel the skin from the kiwi fruit. Reserve a small portion of each fruit. Blend all the fruits together, and serve sprinkled with the chopped fruit. Use a long-handled sundae spoon to eat the fruit from the glass.

Ⓝ 333.4 kcalories • protein 3.020g • carbohydrate 84.90g • fat 2.225g • dietary fiber 10.03g • vit. A 824.9 RE • folate 32.80ug • vit. C 179.6mg • potassium 925mg • calcium 62.10mg.

Cranberry *and Orange*

A reddish-orange juice with a bittersweet taste and a fairly thick texture. A diuretic and cleanser.

Makes approx. 1¾ cups/14 fl. oz.

2 medium oranges
1 cup/4 oz. cranberries
1 tsp. clear honey (optional)

Slice off a small piece of orange for decoration, then peel the remainder, leaving on some of the white pith. Roughly chop, removing seeds if preferred. Wash the cranberries and blend with the orange. Taste the juice; if it is too sour, then sweeten with a little honey. Pour over crushed ice and decorate the glass with the reserved orange slice.

Ⓝ 198.4 kcalories • protein 2.910g • carbohydrate 50.47g • fat 0.534g • dietary fiber 10.91g • vit. A 60.50 RE • folate 81.41ug • vit. C 154.2mg • potassium 555.7mg • calcium 112.9mg.

Grape *and* *Ginger*

Frothy pink in color, and fairly thick in texture, with a sweet, tangy, revitalizing taste. A good cleanser and "pick-me-up."

Makes approx. 1³/₄ cups/14 fl. oz.

1½ cups/6 oz. seedless green grapes
1 ½ cups/6 oz. black grapes
1-in. piece fresh gingerroot

Wash the grapes, and reserve a few for decoration. Remove the pits from the black grapes if preferred. Peel the ginger and roughly chop. Blend the grapes and ginger, and pour into a serving glass. Thread the reserved grapes onto a small skewer, insert into the drink, and serve.

(N) *274.6 kcalories • protein 2.878g • carbohydrate 69.92g • fat 2.050g • dietary fiber 4.260g • vit. A 30.60 RE • folate 17.44ug • vit. C 32.67mg • potassium 807.6mg • calcium 50.07mg.*

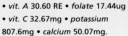
Above Grape and Ginger

Apple *and* *Mint*

A pale-green juice with a refreshing taste. An ideal digestif.

Makes approx. 1¼ cups/½ pint

4 apples
1 lime
Small bunch fresh mint

Wash the apples, core, peel and roughly chop, reserving a slice for decoration. Peel the skin from the lime, leaving the white pith. Wash the mint leaves, and keep a sprig for decoration. Blend or juice. Pour over crushed ice and decorate with reserved apple and mint.

(N) *324.3 kcalories • protein 1.435g • carbohydrate 84.56g • fat 1.920g • dietary fiber 11.60g • vit. A 56.04 RE • folate 38.66ug • vit. C 48.76mg • potassium 722mg • calcium 102.1mg.*

Raspberry *and Strawberry*

A beautiful pink juice, with a mellow, tart taste and thick texture. A cleanser and uplifter.

Makes approx. 1¼ cups/½ pint

1 cup/4 oz. raspberries
1 cup/4 oz. strawberries
1 medium orange

Wash and hull the raspberries and strawberries. Peel the orange, leaving some of the white pith on the orange—remove pits if preferred. Blend all the ingredients together, then pour into a glass and serve with a stirrer.

Ⓝ 166.6 *kcalories • protein* 3.259g • *carbohydrate* 40.10g • *fat* 1.385g • *dietary fiber* 14.93g • *vit. A* 47.97 RE • *folate* 98.10ug • *vit. C* 185mg • *potassium* 671mg • *calcium* 100.4mg.

Melon *and Rosemary*

A pale-peach color with a frothy, pulpy texture. The flavor is fragrant and sweet. Melon juice helps to calm the digestion.

Makes approx. 1¾ cups/14 fl. oz.

¼ honeydew melon
½ cantaloupe
Small bunch of fresh rosemary

Cut the melon into slices and slice off the skin. Remove the pips if preferred and chop roughly. Wash the rosemary and keep a piece for decoration. Blend the melon and rosemary together. Pour into a glass and decorate with reserved rosemary to serve.

Ⓝ 259.1 *kcalories • protein* 4.781g • *carbohydrate* 61.83g • *fat* 2.485g • *dietary fiber* 4.600g • *vit. A* 1069 RE • *folate* 54.40ug • *vit. C* 227.6mg • *potassium* 1989mg • *calcium* 160.7mg.

Right **Melon and Rosemary**

Mango *and* Peach

A golden-orange color with flecks of red; very thick and creamy in texture. You will probably need to dilute this one, or else serve it with a spoon! A good vitality-boosting drink.

Makes approx. 1 cup/8 fl. oz.

1 small or "mini" mango
1 peach
1 lime

Peel the mango, slicing the flesh off the pit, and chop the flesh. Wash and halve the peach and remove the pit. Chop the flesh, reserving a wedge for decoration. Slice off the lime skin leaving some white pith behind. Halve and remove seeds if preferred, reserving a slice for decoration. Blend all the fruit together. Pour into a glass with a few ice cubes. Decorate with a peach wedge and a lime slice.

Ⓝ 249 *kcalories • protein 3.059g • carbohydrate 66.56g • fat 0.890g • dietary fiber 9.760g • vit. A 923.7 RE • folate 12.92ug • vit. C 91.20mg • potassium 821.3mg • calcium 53.70mg.*

Papaya *and* Passionfruit

Peachy-pink color speckled with seeds. A thick, fragrant juice that acts as a cleanser, mild laxative, and good energy booster. It is also very satisfying.

Makes approx. 1¼ cups/½ pint

1 papaya
3 passionfruits
1 lime
Lime leaves to decorate

Cut papaya in half and scoop out the seeds. Peel off the skin, chop the flesh and place in a blender. Halve the passionfruits; put the flesh and seeds of 5 halves in the blender. Peel the lime, halve, and remove pits if preferred. Add to the other fruits and blend together. Pour over crushed ice in a glass. Slice the sixth passionfruit half a little so it sits on the glass, and serve decorated with lime leaves.

Ⓝ 518.7 *kcalories • protein 6.303g • carbohydrate 127.9g • fat 1.665g • dietary fiber 5.882g • vit. A 1824 RE • folate 58.69ug • vit. C 241.0mg • potassium 2489mg • calcium 85.34mg.*

Black Currant *and Apple*

A deep-purple juice with a rich, tart, tangy taste. A strong antioxidant and cleanser.

Makes approx. 1 ¼ cups/½ pint

1 ½ cups/6 oz. black currants
2 apples
1 tsp. honey (optional)
Small bunch of black currants to decorate

Wash black currants thoroughly, pull off the stalks, and place in a blender. Wash the apples, peel, core, roughly chop, and juice. Add the black currants and blend together. Taste and add honey to sweeten if preferred. Pour over ice cubes, decorate the glass with a draped bunch of black currants, and serve.

Ⓝ 291 *kcalories • protein 3.157g • carbohydrate 73.92g • fat 1.599g • dietary fiber 4.874g • vit. A 55.47 RE • folate 1.164ug • vit. C 366.2mg • potassium 926.5mg • calcium 118.7mg.*

Above Black Currant and Apple

Grapefruit, *Orange, and Basil*

A pale, frothy, pink-orange color flecked with green, full of zest and tang. It has a fairly thick, pulpy texture. Rich in vitamin C, it is also a good digestive aid and contributes to healthier skin.

Makes approx. 1 ¼ cups/½ pint

1 pink grapefruit
1 medium orange
Small bunch of basil leaves

Peel the skin from the grapefruit and orange, leaving some of the white pith behind. Halve, remove pits if preferred, chop roughly, and place in blender. Wash the basil, reserving a sprig for decoration, and blend in with the citrus fruits. Alternatively, juice the citrus fruits. Chop the basil separately and stir in to the juices. Serve in a glass decorated with the basil sprig.

Ⓝ 136.1 *kcalories • protein 2.640g • carbohydrate 33.91g • fat 0.418g • dietary fiber 5.850g • vit. A 101.2 RE • folate 64.40ug • vit. C 161.2mg • potassium 560.6mg • calcium 93.15mg.*

Cherry, *Peach, and Pear*

A pale, pinky-orange color, sweet-tasting, and thick-ish in texture. Has strong alkaline content, and is a good cleanser and diuretic.

Makes approx. 1½ cups/12 fl. oz.

1½ cups/6 oz. cherries
1 peach
1 pear

Wash, de-stalk, and pit cherries, reserving a pair for decoration. Wash, halve, stone and roughly chop the peach. Wash the pear, peel, remove the stalk, and core. Blend all the fruits together and serve decorated with reserved cherries.

Ⓝ 251.6 *kcalories • protein* 3.581g • *carbohydrate* 63.11g • *fat* 1.440g • *dietary fiber* 8.510g • *vit. A* 347.3 RE • *folate* 32.46ug • *vit. C* 35.63mg • *potassium* 781mg • *calcium* 59.85mg.

Plum *and Apricot*

A rich, golden juice, thick in texture. An excellent juice to help you on the road to recovery after an illness.

Makes approx. 1½ cups/12 fl. oz.

4 medium plums
4 medium apricots
1 pear
Edible flowers to decorate
  (see page 12)

Wash and halve the plums and apricots, and discard the pits. Pull out the stalk from the pear, peel, and core. Blend all the fruits together. Pour into a glass and decorate.

Ⓝ 245.5 *kcalories • protein* 2.623g • *carbohydrate* 64.78g • *fat* 1.216g • *dietary fiber* 9.720g • *vit. A* 403.7 RE • *folate* 26.72ug • *vit. C* 24.76mg • *potassium* 816mg • *calcium* 50.06mg.

Left **Plum and Apricot**

Carrot, *Orange,* and *Apple*

A bright orange, sunny drink, packed full of get-up-and-go.

Makes approx. 1 1/4 cups/1/2 pint

3 medium carrots
1 medium orange
1 apple

Scrub the carrots well and remove tops. Wash and reserve a few for garnish, and chop roughly. Juice. Cut one slice from the orange and then peel. Remove pits if preferred. Juice. Wash the apple, peel if necessary, core, and then juice. Mix all the juices together. Serve decorated with the reserved carrot tops and orange slice.

Ⓝ *227.6 kcalories • protein 3.648g • carbohydrate 56.30g • fat 0.965g • dietary fiber 12.05g • vit. A 6107 RE • folate 70.51ug • vit. C 94.92mg • potassium 1081mg • calcium 115.7mg.*

Salad *in a* *Glass*

A predominantly green, watery juice with a refreshing, savory flavor. A good juice for the skin; also diuretic and cleansing.

Makes approx. 1 cup/8 fl. oz.

6 lettuce leaves
½ cucumber
1 cup/4 oz. radishes
1 stick celery with leaves
3 scallions
2 medium tomatoes

Wash all the ingredients. Trim the scallions (reserving one for decoration) and celery. Remove the stalks from the tomatoes. Roughly chop all the ingredients, reserving a slice each of cucumber and radish, and blend or juice. Pour into a glass, and serve with a scallion stirrer, a slice of cucumber, and radish.

Ⓝ 144.7 *kcalories • protein* 6.321g • *carbohydrate* 30.96g • *fat* 2.032g • *dietary fiber* 9.610g • *vit. A* 230.1 RE • *folate* 181.7ug • *vit. C* 93.86mg • *potassium* 1462mg • *calcium* 113mg.

Gazpacho

Ruby red-colored, flecked with green. Thick in texture. Good for the circulation and skin, and a diuretic.

Makes approx. 1¼ cups/½ pint

8 medium tomatoes
1 large red bell pepper
1 small onion
1 garlic clove
Small bunch of fresh parsley

Wash the tomatoes, and remove stalks. Wash the bell pepper, halve, remove stalk and seeds, and chop roughly. Peel the onion and garlic. Juice the tomatoes, pepper, onion, and garlic together. Wash the parsley, reserving a sprig for garnish. Chop and mix into the juice. Pour into a glass, add some ice cubes, garnish with parsley and serve.

Ⓝ 272.7 *kcalories • protein* 9.395g • *carbohydrate* 59.75g • *fat* 3.439g • *dietary fiber* 13.36g • *vit. A* 683 RE • *folate* 171.2ug • *vit. C* 261.7mg • *potassium* 2354mg • *calcium* 68.19mg.

Cherry Tomato *and Nectarine*

A tempting, orangey-red color with a fairly sweet taste and a thick, pulpy texture. Good for the circulation and digestion.

Makes approx. 1¾ cups/14 fl. oz.

1½ cups/6 oz. cherry tomatoes
2 medium nectarines

Wash the tomatoes and remove the stalks, reserving one for garnish. Wash the nectarines. Halve, remove the pits, and roughly chop. Blend together and serve. Slit the reserved tomato to sit on the glass.

 168.9 *kcalories* • *protein* 4.011g • *carbohydrate* 39.89g • *fat* 1.812g • *dietary fiber* 6.571g • *vit. A* 307.1 RE • *folate* 35.58ug • *vit. C* 47.20mg • *potassium* 953.2mg • *calcium* 22.11mg.

Herby Tomato

A rich-red juice with flecks of green; a very tasty, savory drink.

Makes approx. 1¼ cups/½ pint

12 medium tomatoes
2 sticks celery
Small bunch of fresh basil
Small bunch of fresh cilantro
Small bunch of fresh chives
1 cherry tomato for decoration

Wash the tomatoes and remove the stalks. Wash and trim the celery. Juice together well. Wash all the herbs, finely chop, and mix into the juice. Pour into a glass and decorate.

(N) 331.9 *kcalories* • *protein* 13.89g • *carbohydrate* 72.43g • *fat* 5.162g • *dietary fiber* 17.81g • *vit. A* 1005 RE • *folate* 248.4ug • *vit. C* 293.9mg • *potassium* 3668mg • *calcium* 131.4mg.

Left **Herby Tomato**

Fennel *and* Orange

A pale, creamy orange juice with a delicious, licorice-like flavor. Has an excellent calming effect, and is a good digestif.

Makes approx. 1¼ cups/½ pint

1 bulb fennel
2 large oranges
Small bunch basil leaves

Wash and trim the fennel, reserving the fronds. Roughly chop. Peel the skin from the oranges, leaving some white pith behind. Save some of the peel to garnish. Roughly chop, discarding pits if preferred. Wash the basil and add into juicer. Juice all the ingredients and serve garnished with fennel fronds and orange peel.

Ⓝ 150.9 *kcalories • protein 3.600g • carbohydrate 37.25g • fat 0.503g • dietary fiber 6.280g • vit. A 75.95 RE • folate 104.5ug • vit. C 150.3mg • potassium 845.6mg • calcium 151.3mg.*

Watercress, *Celery, and Cucumber*

A bright-green juice with a rich, peppery flavor. A strong cleanser; good for the skin.

Makes approx. ¾ cup/⅓ pint

Bunch of watercress—approx.
     ⅓ cup/3 oz.
½ cucumber
4 sticks celery with leaves
Small bunch of chives

Wash the watercress, and reserve a sprig for garnish. Wash the cucumber and roughly chop. Wash and trim the celery, reserving the leaves. Wash the chives and finely chop. Juice all the ingredients together, stir in the chives, and serve garnished with watercress and celery leaves.

Ⓝ 46.78 *kcalories • protein 2.533g • carbohydrate 10.18g • fat 0.440g • dietary fiber 4.086g • vit. A 110 RE • folate 66.44ug • vit. C 24.64mg • potassium 716.8mg • calcium 99.29mg.*

Spinach *and Onion*

A grass-green juice, with a strong, sweet, earthy flavor. A strong stimulating and cleansing tonic. This drink is an excellent source of vitamins A, B1, B3, and B6, and is rich in potassium, calcium, phosphorus, sulfur, and chlorine.

Makes approx. 1¼ cups/½ pint

**1 cup/4 oz. fresh, young spinach
    leaves
2 apples
1 medium onion
Small bunch of parsley**

Wash the spinach well, reserving a leaf for garnish. Wash the apples, core, and peel if preferred. Roughly chop. Peel the onion, chop and add to apples. Wash the parsley well, reserving a small sprig, and finely chop the remainder. Juice all the ingredients together, stir in the chopped parsley, garnish with spinach leaf and parsley sprig, and serve immediately.

Ⓝ *181.8 kcalories • protein 3.874g • carbohydrate 44.20g • fat 1.475g • dietary fiber 8.506g • vit. A 700.6 RE • folate 205.1ug • vit. C 106.9mg • potassium 950.6mg • calcium 152.8mg.*

Sprouting Seed

A pale, watery juice with flecks of bright green; it has a strong, nutty, onion-like flavor. A highly nutritious drink as alfalfa sprouts are one of the most nutritionally valuable plants we can eat.

Makes approx. ¾ cup/⅓ pint

**1 cup/4 oz. alfalfa sprouts
2¼ cups/8 oz. bean sprouts
3 scallions
1 garlic clove**

Wash the sprouts; then trim, and chop two of the scallions and peel the garlic. Juice all the ingredients. Serve, using remaining scallion, trimmed, as a stirrer.

Ⓝ *120.9 kcalories • protein 10.84g • carbohydrate 21.65g • fat 1.259g • dietary fiber 5.946g • vit. A 596 RE • folate 165.9ug • vit. C 67.53mg • potassium 512.2mg • calcium 93.29mg.*

Hot Carrot
and Tomato

A rich-orange color, with a sweet taste and a distinct "kick." A tonic, cleanser, and "pick-up-up."

Makes approx. ¾ cup/⅓ pint

2 medium carrots
8 medium tomatoes
1 garlic clove
1 small red chile

Wash and scrub the carrots, using a vegetable peeler, and shave off some thin ribbons of carrot for a garnish. Roughly chop the remainder. Wash the tomatoes, remove the stalks, reserve a slice, and roughly chop the rest. Peel the garlic, then wash and deseed the chile. Juice all the vegetables together and serve over crushed ice, garnished with carrot ribbons and sliced tomato.

 332.9 *kcalories • protein* 13.08g • *carbohydrate* 75.47g • *fat* 3.837g • *dietary fiber* 17.43g • *vit. A* 4776 RE • *folate* 202.6ug • *vit. C* 566.3mg • *potassium* 3172mg • *calcium* 120.4mg.

Root Vegetable

A pale, creamy orange juice. Cleansing and rejuvenating it aids in reducing excessive uric acid.

Makes approx. ¾ cup/⅓ pint

1 medium parsnip
1 medium turnip
2 medium carrots
1 medium leek

Wash and scrub parsnip, turnip, and carrots. Remove stalk ends and roughly chop. Wash the leek thoroughly. Cut off a small piece of leek and shred, then set aside. Roughly chop the remainder. Juice all the vegetables together, and serve, sprinkled with the shredded leek and garnish with a carrot leaf.

Ⓝ 214.7 *kcalories • protein* 4.929g • *carbohydrate* 51.17g • *fat* 0.943g • *dietary fiber* 11.23g • *vit. A* 4062 RE • *folate* 152.3ug • *vit. C* 47.50mg • *potassium* 1081mg • *calcium* 158mg.

Left Root Vegetable

Spring Vegetable

A bright-green juice, packed full of flavor. A good cleanser and stimulator; rich in vitamin C.

Makes approx. ½ cup/¼ pint

1 cup/4 oz. asparagus spears
1 cup/4 oz. broccoli
1 cup/4 oz. spring cabbage
2 sticks celery
Small bunch of rosemary

Wash all the vegetables and the rosemary, and roughly chop, reserving an asparagus spear. Juice them all together. Finely chop the rosemary and mix into the juice. Serve using reserved asparagus as a stirrer, garnished with rosemary.

 127.6 *kcalories • protein 9.250g • carbohydrate 23.25g • fat 2.409g • dietary fiber 9.180g • vit. A 272.4 RE • folate 362.4ug • vit. C 155.1mg • potassium 1027mg • calcium 251mg.*

Below **Beet, Fennel, and Apple**

Beet, *Fennel,* and *Apple*

A dark-purple, rich, sweet, earthy-tasting juice with a slight licorice flavor. A powerful cleanser.

Makes approx. 1 cup/8 fl. oz.

1 cup/4 oz. fresh beets
1 bulb fennel
2 medium apples

Wash and scrub the beets, and trim tops. Wash and trim fennel, reserving the fronds. Wash the apples, core, peel if preferred. After reserving the apple slice for garnish, roughly chop with the beets and fennel. Juice all the vegetables together, and then serve, garnished with fennel fronds and a slice of apple.

 281 *kcalories • protein 5.104g • carbohydrate 68.94g • fat 1.313g • dietary fiber 12.49g • vit. A 26.46 RE • folate 252.5ug • vit. C 47.74mg • potassium 1447mg • calcium 92.24mg.*

Shakes and Smoothies

While traditional milk shakes are laden with fat and sugar, these healthy drinks taste fantastic, are full of nutrition, and are also low-fat. They can be used to make an excellent light meal—particularly the savory ones—or a simple sustaining snack. Some are lusciously thick, and it is up to your personal taste whether you drink them as they are or dilute them with mineral water or milk—don't forget that the calorie content will be higher if milk is added.

Banana *and Mango Milk*

A thick, creamy shake, low in fat, with a sweet, fragrant flavor. Excellent for enhancing vitality.

Makes approx. 2¼ cups/18 fl. oz.

1 medium mango
1 medium banana
⅔ cup/5 fl. oz. freshly made orange juice
⅔ cup/5 fl. oz. skim milk or soy milk
Orange zest to decorate

Peel the mango and slice the flesh from the pit. Reserve a strip of the skin and a few small cubes of the fruit for decoration. Peel and chop the banana. Place the fruits in a blender along with the orange juice and milk. Blend until smooth, and serve with cubes of mango threaded onto a skewer, interwoven with a strip of mango skin with a sprinkling of orange zest.

Ⓝ *369.3 kcalories • protein 8.633g • carbohydrate 86.96g • fat 1.704g • dietary fiber 7.416g • vit. A 940.8 RE • folate 78.48ug • vit. C 154.9mg • potassium 1350mg • calcium 243.0mg.*

Pineapple *and* Coconut Milk

A sweet, creamy, yellow-colored drink with the decadent taste of coconut, and the rich creaminess of yogurt. Coconut does contain saturated fat, so keep this drink for an occasional treat. It should be avoided if on a strict low-fat/cholesterol diet. However, the drink will give you a real energy boost.

Makes approx. 1¾ cups/14 fl. oz.

½ medium pineapple
2 Tbsp./1 oz. fresh coconut meat
½ cup/5 fl. oz. low-fat natural
**   yogurt**

Peel the pineapple, reserving a thin slice and a leaf for decoration. Chop the remaining pineapple and place in a blender. Dice the coconut meat and place in the blender, adding the yogurt. Blend for a few seconds until smooth. Pour into a glass and serve decorated with a pineapple slice and leaf.

Ⓝ 282.3 *kcalories • protein 7.493g • carbohydrate 51.94g • fat 7.217g • dietary fiber 4.243g • vit. A 24.35 RE • folate 46.44ug • vit. C 48.79mg • potassium 654.6mg • calcium 230.8mg.*

Above Pineapple and Coconut Milk

Banana *and* Pineapple Smoothie

A thick, easy-to-digest energy booster, with a creamy, tangy, sweet taste.

Makes approx. 1¾ cups/14 fl. oz.

1 medium banana
½ medium pineapple
1 lime
Slice of lime to decorate

Peel and chop the banana, and place in the blender. Peel the pineapple, chop, and place in the blender. Peel the lime, chop, discard pits and add to the other fruit. Blend for a few seconds until smooth. Pour into a glass filled with crushed ice, decorate with sliced lime, and serve.

Ⓝ 285.6 *kcalories • protein 3.045g • carbohydrate 75.15g • fat 2.070g • dietary fiber 9.135g • vit. A 16.27 RE • folate 62.41ug • vit. C 85.95mg • potassium 898.2mg • calcium 59.89mg.*

Pear *and Blueberry Lassi*

Traditionally made without fruit to accompany a rich Indian meal, this version adds pear to sweeten naturally. It is a pretty, purpley-pink color, and has a fragrant flavor. It is low in fat and good for the digestion.

Makes approx. 1¾ cups/14 fl. oz.

1 pear
1 cup/4 oz. blueberries
¾ cup/⅓ pt. low-fat, natural, "live" yogurt
2 Tbsp. freshly made lemon juice

Wash the pear, peel, and core. Place in a blender. Wash the blueberries and add to the pear. Add the yogurt and lemon juice. Blend well until smooth, and serve.

(N) *294.7 kcalories • protein 10.66g • carbohydrate 60.24g • fat 3.855g • dietary fiber 8.022g • vit. A 45.66 RE • folate 44.37ug • vit. C 40.81mg • potassium 773.1mg • calcium 340.4mg.*

Avocado Pear *Smoothie*

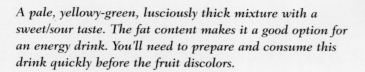

A pale, yellowy-green, lusciously thick mixture with a sweet/sour taste. The fat content makes it a good option for an energy drink. You'll need to prepare and consume this drink quickly before the fruit discolors.

Makes approx. 1¾ cups/14 fl. oz.

1 small, ripe avocado
1 lemon
1 pear
Lemon zest to decorate

Working quickly, peel and stone the avocado, and then place in a blender. Peel the lemon, roughly chop, and discard the pits if preferred. Add to the blender. Wash the pear, peel, core, then add to the blender. Process until smooth. Pour into a glass, decorate, and serve.

(N) *425.1 kcalories • protein 5.025g • carbohydrate 43.47g • fat 30.86g • dietary fiber 12.99g • vit. A 111.4 RE • folate 131.3ug • vit. C 58.78mg • potassium 1394mg • calcium 60.44mg.*

Papaya, *Peach, and Passionfruit* Smoothie

A deliciously fragrant smoothie. A thick, pinky-orange-colored drink speckled with black and red. Low fat, cleansing, and good for the digestion.

Makes 2¼ cups/18 fl. oz.

1 papaya
1 peach
2 passion fruit
⅔ cup/5 fl. oz. freshly made orange juice

Peel the papaya and remove the seeds. Chop and place in a blender. Wash the peach, halve, and remove the pit. Add to the blender. Halve the passionfruit and scoop out the seeds from 3 halves, then add to the blender along with the orange juice. Blend until smooth. Serve poured over ice cubes with the remaining passionfruit over the top, and a stirrer.

(N) *224.3 kcalories • protein 3.770g • carbohydrate 54.76g • fat 0.934g • dietary fiber 9.570g • vit. A 162.0 RE • folate 134.7ug • vit. C 223.8mg • potassium 1146mg • calcium 76.13mg.*

Right **Pear and Blueberry Lassi**

Strawberry
Smoothie

A shake with a sweet berry taste and orangey tang. A good cleanser for the whole body.

Makes approx. 1¾ cups/14 fl. oz.

2¼ cups/8 oz. strawberries
1 large orange

Wash and hull the strawberries. Place all but one in a blender. Peel the orange, leaving some white pith behind, and keep some skin to use for decoration. Chop, remove pits, and place in the blender. Blend until smooth, then pour into a glass, decorated with the reserved strawberry and the orange zest.

Ⓝ *166.4 kcalories • protein 3.356g • carbohydrate 40.25g • fat 1.298g • dietary fiber 10.79g • vit. A 43.32 RE • folate 102.4ug • vit. C 256.1mg • potassium 790.3mg • calcium 107.3mg.*

Mango *and*
Kiwi Lassi

Another yogurt-based drink, which is also very sweet and fragrant. Good for the skin, uplifting, and rich in vitamin C.

Makes approx. 1¾ cups/14 fl. oz.

1 small or "mini" mango
2 kiwi fruits
¾ cup/⅓ pt. low-fat, natural, "live" yogurt
2 Tbsp. freshly made lemon juice

Peel and slice the mango and place in a blender. Peel the kiwi fruits, reserve a slice, and add to the mango. Add the yogurt and lemon juice and blend. Pour into a glass, and float a slice of kiwi fruit on top to serve.

Ⓝ *343.4 kcalories • protein 11.60g • carbohydrate 72.44g • fat 3.867g • dietary fiber 9.012g • vit. A 860.2 RE • folate 22.99ug • vit. C 221.7mg • potassium 1263mg • calcium 373.7mg.*

Left Mango and Kiwi Lassi

Cranberry *and* Apple Shake

A good cleanser and diuretic, add extra sweetener if preferred.

Makes approx. 2 cups/¾ pint

⅔ cup/5 fl. oz. fresh cranberry
  juice
⅔ cup/5 fl. oz. fresh apple juice
⅔ cup/5 fl. oz. low-fat, natural
  yogurt
½ tsp. freshly ground cinnamon
1 tsp. clear honey
**Edible flowers to decorate
  (see page 12)**

Combine the juices, yogurt, and cinnamon. Taste and sweeten with honey if desired. Pour into a glass filled with ice, dust with more cinnamon, and decorate with flowers to serve.

Ⓝ 277.4 *kcalories • protein 7.597g • carbohydrate 57.56g • fat 2.567g • dietary fiber 0.954g • vit. A 22.99 RE • folate 16.49ug • vit. C 58.83mg • potassium 554.1mg • calcium 289.6mg.*

Raspberry *and* Mint Shake

A thick, uplifting drink.

Makes approx. 1¾ cups/14 fl. oz.

**1½ cups/6 oz. raspberries
Small bunch fresh mint
⅔ cup/5 fl. oz. low-fat, natural,
  "live" yogurt
⅔ cup/5 fl. oz. skim milk
1 tsp. clear honey (optional)**

Wash and remove stalks from raspberries and place in a blender. Wash the mint, reserving a sprig for decoration, and place the rest with the raspberries. Add the yogurt and milk, and blend until smooth. Taste and sweeten with honey if preferred and decorate.

Ⓝ 309.9 *kcalories • protein 14.60g • carbohydrate 57.53g • fat 3.688g • dietary fiber 9.087g • vit. A 174.7 RE • folate 103.4ug • vit. C 57.58mg • potassium 950.7mg • calcium 549.5mg.*

Left **Raspberry and Mint Shake**

Cucumber *and* *Mint Cooler*

A refreshing, easy-to-digest drink. A diuretic, and "food" for the skin.

Makes approx. 2½ cups/1 pint

½ cucumber
1 small onion
Small bunch fresh mint
1¼ cups/½ pt. low-fat, natural "live" yogurt

Wash the cucumber; slice off a few pieces for garnish, and then chop the rest. Place in a blender. Peel the onion and place in the blender. Wash the mint, reserve a sprig, and then place the remainder along with the cucumber and onion into the blender. Add the yogurt and blend until smooth. Pour into a glass, and garnish with reserved cucumber and mint.

Ⓝ *213.7 kcalories • protein 16.22g • carbohydrate 26.09g • fat 4.805g • dietary fiber 1.361g • vit. A 114.2 RE • folate 86.27ug • vit. C 20.19mg • potassium 970.5mg • calcium 603.6mg.*

Carrot *and Avocado Smoothie*

A tasty meal in a glass. Good for energy.

Makes approx. 1¾ cups/14 fl. oz.

1 small, ripe avocado
4 Tbsp. freshly made lemon juice
Small bunch chives
½ cup/¼ pt. freshly made carrot juice
⅔ cup/5 fl. oz. low-fat, natural "live" yogurt

Peel and pit the avocado. Chop and place in a blender with the lemon juice. Wash the chives, reserving a few for a garnish, and add to the avocado, along with the carrot juice and yogurt. Blend for a few seconds until smooth, then pour into a glass and snip the reserved chives over the top using a pair of scissors.

Ⓝ *409.8 kcalories • protein 12.49g • carbohydrate 47.09g • fat 22.64g • dietary fiber 13.33g • vit. A 3334 RE • folate 151.0ug • vit. C 58.17mg • potassium 1882mg • calcium 319.1mg.*

Avocado-Salad *Smoothie*

Try this shake for lunch or supper; it's very satisfying and refreshing.

Makes approx. 2¼ cups/18 fl. oz.

1 small, ripe avocado
2 Tbsp. freshly made lemon juice
1 quantity of "Salad In A Glass" Juice (see page 46)
⅔ cup/5 fl. oz. low-fat, natural, "live" yogurt
Small bunch fresh dill
Stick of celery for serving

Peel and pit the avocado. Place in a blender with the lemon juice, salad juice, and yogurt. Wash the dill, reserve some for garnish, and place remainder in blender. Blend until smooth and pour into a glass. Finely chop reserved dill and sprinkle over the drink. Serve using the stick of celery as a stirrer.

Ⓝ *374.3 kcalories • protein 12.71g • carbohydrate 36.92g • fat 22.91g • dietary fiber 12.88g • vit. A 442.0 RE • folate 205.7ug • vit. C 66.22mg • potassium 1860mg • calcium 376.6mg.*

Chile, *Tomato, and Pepper Lassi*

A smooth-tasting drink that is good for both the skin and circulation.

Makes approx. 2 cups/¾ pint

2 small, red chiles
Small bunch of fresh cilantro
⅔ cup/5 fl. oz. freshly made tomato juice
⅔ cup/5 fl. oz. freshly made red pepper juice
⅔ cup/5 fl. oz. low-fat, natural "live" yogurt

Wash the chiles, keeping one aside for garnish. Deseed the remaining chile and chop finely. Wash the cilantro and roughly chop, reserving a small amount for the garnish. Place the chopped chile and cilantro in a blender along with the tomato juice, pepper juice, and yogurt. Blend until smooth. Pour over crushed ice. Float the chopped cilantro on top to serve.

(N) *183.2 kcalories • protein 12.62g • carbohydrate 27.08g • fat 3.272g • dietary fiber 7.487g • vit. A 2134 RE • folate 58.94ug • vit. C 357.7mg • potassium 1297mg • calcium 261.3mg.*

Cocktails and Punches

If you're stuck for ideas to serve at a party or social gathering, then look no further. This chapter has flavorsome nonalcoholic drinks aplenty, all with a healthy twist. The recipes each serve one, but can easily be doubled or tripled to suit the occasion.

Pineapple-Mint *Julep*

An unusual combination, but delicious. Should be served over ice to be truly enjoyed.

Makes approx. 1 1/2 cups/12 fl. oz.

1 peppermint-tea bag
2/3 cup/5 fl. oz. boiling water
1/4 medium pineapple
Small bunch of fresh mint
Few ice cubes

Place the tea bag in a small, heat-proof jug and pour over the boiling water. Leave to infuse for 5 minutes, discard bag, then allow to cool. Just before serving, peel the pineapple, and blend or juice. Wash and roughly chop the mint. Place ice cubes in a serving glass and pour over the pineapple juice, chopped mint, and cooled tea. Mix well and serve with a cocktail stirrer.

Ⓝ 101.6 kcalories • *protein* 1.002g • *carbohydrate* 22.55g • *fat* 1.072g • *dietary fiber* 1.860g • *vit. A* 72.88 RE • *folate* 84.81ug • *vit. C* 41.47mg • *potassium* 366.3mg • *calcium* 129.8mg.

Virgin Mary

A classic at any cocktail party. The amount of Worcestershire and Tabasco sauces you add is up to your personal taste.

Makes approx. ¾ cup/⅓ pint

8 medium tomatoes
½ lemon
Dash of Worcestershire sauce
Dash of Tabasco sauce
Few celery leaves, washed, and
    chopped
Stick of celery, washed and
    trimmed

Wash the tomatoes and remove stalks. Roughly chop and place in a blender. Peel the lemon, remove the pits if preferred, roughly chop, and add to the tomatoes. Blend for a few seconds until smooth. Add sauces to taste, and then serve with or without ice. Sprinkle with chopped celery leaves and serve with a stick of celery as a stirrer.

ⓝ 239 *kcalories • protein 9.975g • carbohydrate 56.53g • fat 3.522g • dietary fiber 12.16g • vit. A 629.3 RE • folate 170.2ug • vit. C 258.9mg • potassium 2585mg • calcium 125.7mg.*

Above Virgin Mary

Sparkling Cranberry and Orange

A cooling, refreshing cocktail with a slight fizz.

Makes approx. 2¼ cups/18 fl. oz.

1 quantity (1¾ cups) Cranberry
    and Orange Juice (see page 38)
Few ice cubes
Chilled, carbonated mineral water
Few slices of fresh orange

Pour the juice into a blender. Add the ice cubes and blend until well crushed. Gently mix in sufficient carbonated mineral water as desired, and serve immediately with orange slices to float.

ⓝ 337.2 *kcalories • protein 3.780g • carbohydrate 84.84g • fat 0.782g • dietary fiber 11.15g • vit. A 85.30 RE • folate 119ug • vit. C 216mg • potassium 804mg • calcium 129.1mg.*

Exotic Fruit Piña Colada

Traditionally made with rum, this thick, creamy cocktail is so packed with fruity flavors and coconut, you won't miss it.

Makes approx. 2¼ cups/18 fl. oz.

¼ medium pineapple
½ papaya
2 passionfruits
1 oz. fresh coconut meat
Chilled mineral water
Scoop of crushed ice
Fresh coconut flakes

Peel and roughly chop the pineapple. Peel the papaya, scoop out the seeds, and roughly chop. Place in a blender. Halve the passionfruits, then scoop out the flesh and seeds and put into the blender. Grate the coconut meat into the blender as well. Blend for a few seconds until smooth. Add mineral water as desired. Pile the ice into a serving glass and pour over the blended fruit. Serve decorated with fresh coconut flakes.

Ⓝ 424.2 *kcalories* • *protein* 3.737g • *carbohydrate* 65.90g • *fat* 19.42g • *dietary fiber* 10.44g • *vit. A* 67.50 RE • *folate* 73.78ug • *vit. C* 121.6mg • *potassium* 833.9mg • *calcium* 56.43mg.

Strawberry and Banana Daiquiri

This velvety-smooth cocktail will be a guaranteed favorite, and should be served with traditional cocktail accessories for maximum effect.

Makes approx. 1¼ cups/½ pint

1 medium banana
7 strawberries
1 lime
1 tsp. clear honey (optional)
Scoop of crushed ice

Peel the banana and chop roughly. Place in a blender. Wash the strawberries, keeping one aside for decoration, then remove stalks and place in a blender. Peel the lime, roughly chop, and remove pits. Add to the blender. Process the ingredients until smooth. Taste and sweeten with honey if preferred. Pile crushed ice in a serving glass, pour over daiquiri, and decorate the glass with the reserved strawberry and cocktail accessories.

Ⓝ 235.8 *kcalories* • *protein* 3.478g • *carbohydrate* 60.53g • *fat* 1.783g • *dietary fiber* 11.49g • *vit. A* 18.73 RE • *folate* 80.23ug • *vit. C* 198.9mg • *potassium* 1016mg • *calcium* 71.16mg.

Right **Exotic Fruit Piña Colada**

Spiced-Orange *Punch*

A tangy punch with comforting spices. You can also serve this drink as a hot toddy.

Makes approx. 1½ cups/12 fl. oz.

1 orange fruit-tea bag
2 cloves
1 small piece of cinnamon
⅔ cup/5 fl. oz. boiling water
¾ cup/⅓ pt. freshly made
  orange juice
Few ice cubes
Slice of orange to decorate

Place the tea bag in a heat-proof jug with the cloves and small piece of cinnamon. Pour over the boiling water and leave to infuse for 5 minutes. Remove the bag, leaving the spices, and allow to cool. Then discard the spices. To serve, pour the orange juice into a serving glass over the ice, then add the tea, decorate with a slice of orange, and serve.

(N) *295.3 kcalories • protein 4.896g • carbohydrate 53.13g • fat 7.630g • dietary fiber 7.416g • vit. A 75.25 RE • folate 75.83ug • vit. C 124.7mg • potassium 1063mg • calcium 478.7mg.*

Berry *Sherbet*

If preferred the egg can be left out, but the result will be more icy.

Makes approx. 2¼ cups/18 fl. oz.

1 medium egg white (see note, page 4)
1 quantity (1¼ cups) of Mixed-Berry Juice (see page 36)
1 tsp. clear honey (optional)

Whisk the egg white until thick and frothy, but not stiff. Pour the juice into a blender, add a few ice cubes and egg white. Blend for a few seconds until slushy and foaming. Taste and sweeten with honey if necessary. Pour into a glass, and serve immediately.

(N) *236 kcalories • protein 6.441g • carbohydrate 56.61g • fat 0.534g • dietary fiber 10.91g • vit. A 60.50 RE • folate 82.54ug • vit. C 154mg • potassium 607.4mg • calcium 115.4mg.*

Above Berry Sherbet

Raspberry *and* Rose Punch

A perfect summer evening drink.

Makes approx. 1³⁄4 cups/14 fl. oz.

1 rosehip-tea bag
²⁄3 cup/5 fl. oz. boiling water
1 cup/4 oz. raspberries
1 tsp.clear honey (optional)
²⁄3 cup/5 fl. oz. carbonated
   mineral water
1 tsp. rose water
Few ice cubes
Few rose petals, to decorate

Place the tea bag in a heat-proof jug and pour over the water. Leave to infuse for 5 minutes, discard bag, then set aside to cool. Wash and hull the raspberries in a blender with the cooled tea and blend until smooth. Taste and sweeten with honey if necessary. Mix in the water and rose water. Place the ice cubes into a serving glass and pour over the punch. Serve with rose petals to float.

Ⓝ *139.6 kcalories • protein 1.368g • carbohydrate 34.60g • fat 0.712g • dietary fiber 6.271g • vit. A 16.28 RE • folate 38.30ug • vit. C 35.47mg • potassium 248.3mg • calcium 29.61mg.*

Mulled Grape and Apple Punch

Similar to mulled wine, this combination of fruit and spices is just the thing to warm you up on a cold day. Try to avoid heating the juices, as this will destroy some of the nutrients.

Makes approx. 1½ cups/12 fl. oz.

1 apple tea bag
2 cloves
1 small piece of cinnamon
⅔ cup/5 fl. oz. boiling water
¼ tsp. freshly grated nutmeg
⅓ cup/3½ fl. oz. freshly made apple juice
⅓ cup/3½ fl. oz. freshly made grape juice
Apple slices

Place the tea bag in a small, heat-proof jug, and then add the cloves and piece of cinnamon. Pour over the water, leave to infuse for 5 minutes, then discard the tea bag and spices. Sprinkle the nutmeg over the tea, and mix into the juices. Pour into a hot, heat-proof glass, and serve with a cinnamon stick stirrer and apple slices to float.

Ⓝ *213.4 kcalories • protein 2.509g • carbohydrate 41.98g • fat 8.423g • dietary fiber 11.35g • vit. A 15.65 RE • folate 33.38ug • vit. C 37.30mg • potassium 501.3mg • calcium 220.8mg.*

Lemon *and* Ginger Fizz

This drink will give you a lift; it's full of zest and flavor.

Makes approx. 1½ cups/12 fl. oz.

1-in. piece gingerroot
⅓ cup/3½ fl. oz. boiling water
1 tsp. clear honey
⅓ cup/3½ fl. oz. freshly made lemon juice
Few ice cubes
⅔ cup/5 fl. oz. carbonated mineral water
Sliced lemon to decorate

Peel and slice the ginger. Place in a heat-proof jug and pour the boiling water over it. Leave aside to infuse for 10 minutes, then discard the ginger and allow to cool. Mix the honey and lemon juice into the cooled ginger water. Pour into a glass filled with ice cubes, and add mineral water to fill. Decorate with lemon slices and serve.

(N) 159.4 *kcalories • protein 3.418g • carbohydrate* 45.13g • *fat 1.175g • dietary fiber 1.788g • vit. A* 4.865 RE • *folate 10.63ug • vit. C 125.0mg • potassium* 367.9mg • *calcium 88.02mg.*

Fennel *and Tomato Warmer*

A soothing, tasty drink that could make a perfect between-meal snack.

Makes approx. 1½ cups/12 fl. oz.

1 fennel tea bag
1 tsp. fennel seeds
¾ cup/⅓ pt. boiling water
⅔ cup/5 fl. oz. freshly made tomato juice
½ Tbsp. freshly chopped dill

Place the tea bag in a hot mug, add the seeds, and pour boiling water over the mixture. Leave to infuse for 5 minutes and discard the tea bag. Mix in the tomato juice. Stir and sprinkle with chopped dill to serve.

(N) 33.69 *kcalories • protein 1.480g • carbohydrate* 7.614g • *fat 0.406g • dietary fiber 1.019g • vit. A* 91.36 RE • *folate 31.81ug • vit. C 12.76mg • potassium* 378.4mg • *calcium 41.89mg.*

Right Fennel and Tomato Warmer

Watermelon *Crush*

On a summer's day there is nothing as refreshing as a slice of watermelon and this cooling, relaxing drink uses watermelon juice as its base—it's just right for a hot day!

Makes approx. 2½ cups/1 pint

**¼ small watermelon or one
    4-in. wedge**
1 lime
Few ice cubes
1 tsp. honey (optional)
½ tsp. freshly ground cinnamon

Reserve a sliver of watermelon for decoration, then peel the rest and chop. Peel the lime and roughly chop, removing pits if preferred. Place the melon and lime in a blender with the ice cubes, honey (if using) and cinnamon. Blend well until slushy. Pile into a serving glass, garnish with reserved watermelon, and serve.

(N) 146.8 *kcalories • protein 2.519g • carbohydrate 36.75g • fat 1.547g • dietary fiber 4.119g • vit. A 119.4 RE • folate 12.67ug • vit. C 50.66mg • potassium 449.7mg • calcium 62.27mg.*

St. Clement's *Cocktail*

This tangy, zesty drink is a classic combination of citrus juices—orange and lemon—with the added zip of pink grapefruit. If the flavor is a little tart for your liking, you can add honey to sweeten.

Makes approx. 1¾ cups/14 fl. oz.

2 medium oranges
½ pink grapefruit
1 lemon
1 tsp. clear honey (optional)
Few ice cubes
**⅔ cup/5 fl. oz. carbonated
    mineral water**

Slice off a small piece of each of the fruits to serve. Peel the oranges, grapefruit, and lemon. Roughly chop and remove the pits if preferred. Place in blender and blend for a few seconds until smooth. Taste and sweeten if liked. Place the ice cubes in a serving glass and pour over the juice. Add the mineral water, and serve with the reserved fruit to float and a cocktail stirrer to mix.

(N) 250.2 *kcalories • protein 3.794g • carbohydrate 64.58g • fat 0.611g • dietary fiber 9.269g • vit. A 88.74 RE • folate 97.24ug • vit. C 215.6mg • potassium 713.6mg • calcium 140.3mg.*

Right **Watermelon Crush**

High-Energy Drinks and Tonics

If you want to build yourself up, replenish your body after a bout of exercise, or even help you to calm down, then these recipes are just what you need.

Vitality Shake

A good energy provider.

Makes approx. 2 cups/¾ pint

1¼ cups/½ pt. skim milk
⅔ cup/5 fl. oz. low-fat, natural yogurt
1 small egg (optional, see note, page 4)
1 to 2 tsp. powdered Brewers' yeast
1 to 2 tsp. clear honey
½ tsp. freshly grated nutmeg, plus extra for dusting
2 tsp. wheat germ

Place the milk, yogurt, egg (if using), yeast, honey, and nutmeg in a blender and mix together. Pour into a serving glass and sprinkle with wheat germ, then dust with more nutmeg to serve.

(N) 311.8 kcalories • protein 24.28g • carbohydrate 37.51g • fat 7.375g • dietary fiber 1.305g • vit. A 280.7 RE • folate 115.2ug • vit. C 4.190mg • potassium 962.1mg • calcium 662.6mg.

Sprouting-Seed *Energy Booster*

This savory shake will provide vitality, is very fresh in taste, and is easy to digest.

Makes approx. 2¼ cups/18 fl. oz.

1 small, ripe avocado
1 lime
⅔ cup/5 fl. oz. low-fat, natural yogurt
1 quantity (¾ cups/⅓ pt.) of Sprouting Seed Juice (see page 49)
1 bunch fresh cilantro

Peel the avocado and discard the pit. Roughly chop and place in a blender. Peel the lime, reserving some for decoration, roughly chop, discard the pits if preferred, and place in the blender with the yogurt and juice. Wash the cilantro and add to the blender—reserve a sprig for decoration. Blend all the ingredients together until smooth. Pour into a serving glass and serve with lime zest and a sprig of fresh cilantro.

Ⓝ *378.3 kcalories • protein 12.36g • carbohydrate 39.24g • fat 22.80g • dietary fiber 14.24g • vit. A 368.5 RE • folate 146.8ug • vit. C 50.06mg • potassium 1576mg • calcium 326.2mg.*

Above Sprouting-Seed Energy Booster

Yeasty-Orange *"Pick-me-up"*

Brewers' yeast has a strong flavor, so the tang of orange is the perfect disguise. An excellent drink for convalescence.

Makes approx. 2 cups/¾ pint

1¼ cups/½ pt. freshly made orange juice
1 to 2 tsp. powdered Brewers' yeast
⅔ cup/5 fl. oz. low-fat, natural yogurt
2 tsp. clear honey
Orange peel to decorate

Mix together the orange juice, Brewers' yeast, yogurt, and honey to taste. Pour into a glass and serve decorated with orange peel.

Ⓝ *282.5 kcalories • protein 10.24g • carbohydrate 55.78g • fat 2.832g • dietary fiber 1.706g • vit. A 87.21 RE • folate 164.0ug • vit. C 164.4mg • potassium 997.2mg • calcium 306.8mg.*

Almond-Seed *"Milk"*

This "milk" is a good source of protein and can be drunk by those on a dairy-free diet. It is delicious drunk with ice.

Makes approx. 1¼ cups/½ pint

¼ cup/1 oz. whole shelled almonds
1 Tbsp. pumpkin seeds
½ tsp. caraway seeds
½ tsp. cumin seeds
1¼ cups/½ pt. mineral water
1 tsp. clear honey
Few ice cubes (optional)
Extra caraway and cumin seeds to sprinkle

Grind the almonds, pumpkin, caraway, and cumin seeds together until very fine in order to obtain a good blend. Transfer to a small jug and gradually blend in the water. Taste and sweeten as desired. Pour into a glass, over ice if liked, and sprinkle with extra seeds.

Ⓝ 216.9 *kcalories • protein* 10.21g *• carbohydrate* 11.68g *• fat* 17.26g *• dietary fiber* 3.137g *• vit. A* 2.444 RE *• folate* 22.43ug *• vit. C* 0.471mg *• potassium* 183.6mg *• calcium* 80.51mg.

Banana-and-Avocado *Smoothie*

A lusciously thick, decadent drink that is a real treat.

Makes approx. 2½ cups/1 pint

1 medium banana
1 small ripe avocado
1 lemon
1 tsp. clear honey
1¼ cups/½ pt. skim milk
2 tsp. wheat germ

Peel and roughly chop the banana. Peel the avocado, discard the pit, roughly chop, and place both banana and avocado in a blender. Slice a piece of lemon and set aside for decoration. Peel the remaining lemon, roughly chop, and discard the pits if preferred. Blend, along with the honey and milk, until smooth. Pour into a serving glass, sprinkle with wheat germ, and decorate.

Ⓝ 550.2 *kcalories • protein* 17.77g *• carbohydrate* 55.85g *• fat* 34.04g *• dietary fiber* 30.51g *• vit. A* 214.9 RE *• folate* 57.60ug *• vit. C* 63.64mg *• potassium* 2393mg *• calcium* 430.4mg.

Oatmeal-and-Raspberry
Smoothie

A thick, nutritious shake with a good dietary-fiber content from the added oatmeal and wheat bran.

Makes approx. 2¼ cups/18 fl. oz.

1½ cups/6 oz. raspberries
⅔ cup/5 fl. oz. freshly made
orange juice
⅔ cup/5 fl. oz. low-fat, natural
yogurt
⅜ cup/1½ oz. fine oatmeal
1 to 2 tsp. clear honey
1 to 2 tsp. wheat bran
Orange zest to decorate

Wash and hull the raspberries and place in a blender with the orange juice, yogurt, and oatmeal. Blend until smooth. Taste and sweeten as desired. Pour into a glass, sprinkle with wheat bran, decorate with orange zest, and serve.

Ⓝ *294.4 kcalories • protein 11.54g • carbohydrate 56.94g • fat 3.989g • dietary fiber 11.21g • vit. A 81.01 RE • folate 115.3ug • vit. C 132.9mg • potassium 974.1mg • calcium 331.1mg.*

Wheat Germ and Berry *Shake*

Creamy smooth in texture, this drink has excellent uplifting properties—it's guaranteed to make you feel good!

Makes approx. 2¼ cups/18 fl. oz.

**1 quantity (1 ¼ cups) of Mixed-
Berry Juice (see page 36)**
¾ cup/⅓ pt. skim milk
2 Tbsp. ground almonds
1 Tbsp. wheat germ
1 to 2 tsp. clear honey

Simply blend together the juice, milk, almonds, and all but one teaspoon wheat germ. Taste and add honey to sweeten as desired. Pour into a glass, sprinkle with the remaining wheat germ, and serve.

Ⓝ *426.9 kcalories • protein 14.68g • carbohydrate 69.84g • fat 14.32g • dietary fiber 14.32g • vit. A 97.75 RE • folate 123.1ug • vit. C 154.7mg • potassium 816.9mg • calcium 251.8mg.*

Sesame and Cinnamon *Shake*

A protein-rich drink, which could make a light meal if accompanied with some fresh fruit.

Makes approx. 1 ½ cups/12 fl. oz.

1 Tbsp. sesame seeds
**¼ cup/1 oz. whole shelled
almonds**
⅔ cup/5 fl. oz. skim milk
⅔ cup/5 fl. oz. low-fat yogurt
½ tsp. ground cinnamon
1 to 2 tsp. clear honey
Few ice cubes (optional)
Toasted sesame seeds to sprinkle
Cinnamon stick to stir

Grind the sesame seeds and almonds together until fine. Transfer to a small jug and blend in the milk, yogurt, and cinnamon. Mix well. Taste and sweeten with the honey. Pour into a glass with ice and sprinkle with the toasted seeds. Add the cinnamon stick to mix.

Ⓝ *426.4 kcalories • protein 21.97g • carbohydrate 30.04g • fat 25.51g • dietary fiber 5.912g • vit. A 116.4 RE • folate 47.48ug • vit. C 3.152mg • potassium 874.0mg • calcium 644.0mg.*

Right **Wheat Germ and Berry Shake**

Soothing Chamomile Toddy

The flowers of chamomile are well recognized for their relaxing and calming properties. When mixed with fruit, this drink is very soothing to the body.

Makes approx. 2½ cups/1 pint

1 chamomile tea bag
¾ cup/⅓ pt. boiling water
1 quantity (1¾ cups) of Grape-and-Ginger Juice (see page 39)

Place the chamomile tea bag in a heated mug and pour in the boiling water. Leave to infuse for 5 minutes, then discard the bag. Pour in the juice and serve immediately.

Ⓝ *277.1 kcalories • protein 2.880g • carbohydrate 70.31g • fat 2.064g • dietary fiber 4.260g • vit. A 30.60 RE • folate 18.65ug • vit. C 32.70mg • potassium 826.6mg • calcium 54.24mg.*

Above Lemon and Honey Toddy with Bee Pollen

Lemon and Honey Toddy *with Bee Pollen*

If you're feeling a bit low, then this comforting drink will help revitalize your system. Try it if you're suffering with a cold or flu.

Makes approx. 1 cup/8 fl. oz.

1 lemon tea bag
¾ cup/⅓ pt. boiling water
1 lemon
1 to 2 tsp. clear honey
2 tsp. bee pollen grains

Place the lemon tea bag in a heated mug and pour in the boiling water. Leave to infuse for 5 minutes.

Discard the bag. Meanwhile, peel the lemon, reserving a slice for decoration, remove pits if preferred, and juice. Stir juice into lemon tea along with the honey and bee pollen grains. Pour and serve with a slice of lemon to float.

Ⓝ *53.06 kcalories • protein 2.757g • carbohydrate 17.48g • fat 0.631g • dietary fiber 0.469g • vit. A 3.240 RE • folate 1.263ug • vit. C 86.22mg • potassium 190mg • calcium 74.94mg.*

Vegetable *Stress-Buster*

Take a break and calm frazzled nerves with this savory treat.

Makes approx. 2¼ cups/18 fl. oz.

½ tsp. bouillon powder
¾ cup/⅓ pt. boiling water
1 quantity (1¼ cups) of Fennel
**   and Orange Juice (see page 48)**
1 small celery stick
4 radish

Place the bouillon powder in a hot mug and pour over the boiling water. Mix well and stir in the juice. Wash and chop the celery and radish and add to the drink. Serve immediately with a spoon.

Below **Vitamin C Tonic**

Ⓝ 165.5 *kcalories • protein* 4.008g *• carbohydrate* 39.81g *• fat* 0.655g *• dietary fiber* 7.248g *• vit. A* 81.28 RE *• folate* 120.1ug *• vit. C* 156.9mg *• potassium* 1002mg *• calcium* 170.8mg.

Vitamin C *Tonic*

Guaranteed to make you feel better.

Makes approx. 2¼ cups/18 fl. oz.

1 quantity (1 cup) of Citrus juice
**   (see page 37)**
1 pink grapefruit
1 tsp. clear honey (optional)
Scoop of crushed ice
⅔ cup/5 fl. oz. carbonated
**   mineral water**

Pour the Citrus juice into a blender. Peel the grapefruit, chop, remove pits if preferred, and add to blender. Blend until smooth. Taste and sweeten with honey if liked. Mix the water and juice, and pour over ice.

Ⓝ 332.7 *kcalories • protein* 4.321g *• carbohydrate* 78.69g *• fat* 1.246g *• dietary fiber* 4.944g *• vit. A* 65 RE *• folate* 23.24ug *• vit. C* 363mg *• potassium* 315.6mg *• calcium* 115.9mg.

Lemon-Barley *Posset Drink*

Traditionally, a posset has a consistency of a watery porridge. The pearl barley used is very soothing if stressed, and nourishing if convalescing.

Makes approx. 1¼ cups/½ pint

¼ cup/1 oz. pearl barley
2½ cups/1 pt. mineral water
1 unwaxed lemon, washed
1 to 2 tsp. clear honey
Lemon zest to decorate

Rinse the barley under cold running water, then place in a saucepan. Pour in the mineral water. Using a vegetable peeler, cut off the lemon zest and add to the saucepan—keep a strip for decoration. Bring to a boil, partially cover, and reduce to a gentle simmer. Cook for 30 minutes until the barley is soft. Cover and set aside to cool. Discard the lemon zest, then transfer the cooked barley and the liquid to a blender. Juice the lemon and add to the cooled barley water, then blend until smooth. Sweeten to taste with the honey, and serve decorated with reserved lemon zest.

Note: for maximum benefit, the posset should be drunk as it is with the sediment. However, if preferred, it can be strained.

Ⓝ *131.6 kcalories • protein 3.545g • carbohydrate 31.22g • fat 0.521g • dietary fiber 6.686g • vit. A 2.607 RE • folate 12.74ug • vit. C 38.46mg • potassium 170.8mg • calcium 31.57mg.*

Japanese Green Tea and Ginseng

Green tea is produced without fermentation and contains very few, if any, chemicals. It is good for the digestion, although it does contain some caffeine. Combined with ginseng, it is a good tonic and "pick-me-up."

Makes approx. 2 cups/¾ pint

1 tsp. Japanese green tea
¾ cup/⅓ pt. boiling water
1 lime
1 tsp. clear honey
500 to 1500 mg. Korean ginseng extract—see manufacturer's dosage label (the extract should come with its own measuring spoon, or be in ready-made capsule doses)

Wedge of lime and an edible flower (see page 12) to decorate

Place the tea in a heat-proof jug and pour in the boiling water. Leave to infuse for 3 minutes and strain into a hot mug. Peel the lime, remove pits if preferred, and juice. Stir into the green tea, adding honey, and ginseng. Decorate with the lime and flower, and serve immediately.

Ⓝ Nutritional analysis not available.

Bibliography

Blauer, Stephen. *The Juicing Book.* New York: Avery Publishing Group, 1989.

Carper, Jean. *The Food Pharmacy.* London: Positive Paperbacks (Simon & Schuster), 1990.

Griggs, Barbara and Van Straten, Michael. *Superfoods.* London: Dorling Kindersley, 1990.

Holland, B., Unwin, I.D., and Buss, D.H. *Fruit and Nuts* - the first supplement to McCance and

Widdowson's *The Composition of Foods (Fifth Edition).* Cambridge: RSC/MAFF, 1992.

Holland, B., Unwin, I. D., and Buss, D.H. *Vegetables, Herbs and Spices* - the fifth supplement to McCance and Widdowsons's *The Composition of Foods (Fourth Edition).* Cambridge: RSC/MAFF, 1991.

Hunt, Jenny. *The Green Cook's Encyclopedia.* London: Green Print, 1991.

Mayes, Adrienne, Ph.D. *The Dictionary of Nutritional Health.* Northampton: Thorsons, 1986.

Walker, N. W., D.Sc. *Fresh Vegetable and Fruit Juices.* Arizona: Norwalk Press, 1978.

Yudkin, John. *The Penguin Encyclopedia of Nutrition.* Middlesex: Viking, 1985.

Index